CROSS WAYS®

2 SECTION

UNITS 11–20

From the Conquest to the Babylonian Exile

Fourth Edition

Harry Wendt

CROSSWAYS INTERNATIONAL
Minneapolis, MN

CROSSWAYS®—SECTION 2

was developed and written by
Harry Wendt, Minneapolis, MN

Illustrations by
Knarelle Beard, Adelaide, South Australia

The Bible text in this publication is from the New Revised Standard Version of the Bible,
copyright 1989 by the Division of Christian Education of the National Council of
Churches of Christ in the United States of America and used by permission.

CROSSWAYS®—SECTION 2

is published and distributed by
CROSSWAYS INTERNATIONAL
7930 Computer Avenue South
Minneapolis, MN 55435
www.crossways.org

ISBN 1-891245-19-8

Fourth Edition

10 9 8 7 6 5 4 3 2

We at Crossways International (CI) are delighted that you are about to undertake a study of the entire sweep of the Old and New Testaments using our materials as your guide. May your journey be fruitful and rewarding, and draw you ever closer to the mind, manner, and meaning of Jesus, the Servant-Messiah.

CI is more than a publisher of Christian education and Bible study materials. We also offer hands-on training in the use of our materials, and we make our materials available to special ministries and missions all around the world. We would be happy to partner with you in *any way* that might help you to share the Good News of God's Kingdom with the people you reach.

The courses of Crossways International have been translated into dozens of languages and are used by all major Christian denominations in numerous countries around the world. We have trained tens of thousands of pastors, teachers, and lay-people to teach the Bible with joy and passion.

WHAT DISTINGUISHES CROSSWAYS INTERNATIONAL?

① A Panoramic View of Scripture

CI's courses examine the meaning of the Bible by digging into the *complete story* that runs through it—from *Genesis to Revelation*. We believe you cannot fully grasp the enormity and profundity of Jesus the Messiah's mind and message without understanding what preceded Him and set the stage for His ministry and mission.

② Visual Learning

All of CI's teaching materials make extensive use of specially designed *color graphics* to help people better understand and remember the written material. These make it easier to share God's Good News.

③ Focus on Jesus, the Servant-King

We are not about biblical study merely for study's sake. The core of every CI course is *Jesus, the King who washed feet*—the Messiah who invites us to follow Him by loving and serving others—as He did. These courses help to *transform hearts and lives*.

④ Tools for Faith Development

CI offers *survey courses of increasing depth* that lead people through the entire story of the Bible—plus *short courses* on specific biblical topics, such as Jesus' parables, Christian stewardship, prayer, the Passion and the Christmas stories.

⑤ Workshop Training for Teachers & Laity

For those interested in *revitalizing their ministries* using CI's courses, we offer workshops that train attendees, step-by-step, how to do it. We also offer workshops for lay-people who are eager to boost their biblical literacy and steep themselves in Scripture. Call us or visit our website.

⑥ Mission Around the World—and at Home

CI's dedication to the mission and message of Jesus goes beyond mere publishing and teacher-training. We make our materials available in the U.S. and all around the world in *prisons, hospitals, orphanages, street ministries*—anywhere the need is great but resources are scarce. CI is a *non-profit ministry* that relies on our modest sales and the benevolence of supporters in our efforts to heed the Great Commission to "go and make disciples of all nations."

Contact Crossways International at 1-800-257-7308 or visit our website at <u>www.crossways.org</u>.

The Structure of the *Crossways* Series

Crossways is offered in six sections of ten units each. Although each section is available for separate purchase, would-be students of the Bible are encouraged to work through all six sections in sequence to gain an overview of the Bible's "big picture." If they choose not to do that, they should first work through a course that will give them an overview of the biblical story-line, such as Crossways International's *See Through the Scriptures* or *The Divine Drama—The Biblical Narrative*. The six sections of *Crossways* are:

From Creation to the Transjordan

Creation; the biblical overture; the patriarchal narratives; the Exodus from Egypt; the Sinai covenant and the Pentateuchal law-codes; the wilderness wanderings.

From the Conquest to the Babylonian Exile

The narratives in Joshua, Judges, 1 and 2 Samuel, 1 and 2 Kings; Worship and Holy War.

The Preexilic and Exilic Prophets

Introducing the Prophets; Amos; Hosea; Isaiah 1–39; Micah; Jeremiah; Nahum, Habakkuk, Zephaniah; Ezekiel.

The Postexilic Period and Judaism

The return from Babylon; the history of the intertestamental period; 1 and 2 Chronicles, Ezra, and Nehemiah; the postexilic prophets; Psalms; Wisdom literature; apocalyptic writings and Daniel, the Apocrypha and Pseudepigrapha; messianic expectations.

The Gospels and Acts

First-century Judaism; Mark; Matthew; Luke; John; Acts.

The Letters and Revelation

Paul and his letters; the Catholic letters; Revelation

CROSS WAYS

2 SECTION

UNITS 11–20

From the Conquest to the Babylonian Exile

UNIT 11

Deuteronomy

The Structure, Themes, and Influence of Deuteronomy

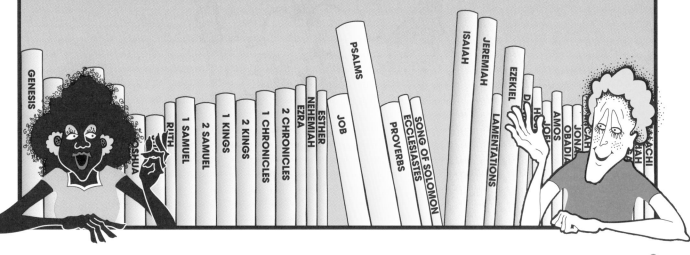

**The land
The Lord alone
One sanctuary
Blessings and curses
Choose life today**

The first five books of the Old Testament (Genesis, Exodus, Leviticus, Numbers, Deuteronomy) are referred to as the *Pentateuch* ("five books"). Although tradition suggests that they were written by Moses, they contain no reference to Moses actually writing them.

Exodus 19:1 reports Israel's *arrival* at Mt. Sinai; Numbers 10:11–13 refers to Israel's *departure* from Sinai. The materials between these two passages focus on the events that took place *at Sinai*. Because the latter chapters of Numbers describe the Israelites destroying enemy nations on the East Bank of the Jordan River, one might expect the next book, Deuteronomy, to report the conquest of Canaan—but it does not.

 ILLUSTRATION 11A summarizes Deuteronomy's content. The setting is the East Bank of the Jordan River. **Moses** is preaching a final sermon to the Israelites who are now preparing to enter and take possession of the Promised Land. Moses' message is based on the themes of the ***Sinai covenant***.

Deuteronomy 1:1 and 1:5 state that Moses delivered this farewell exhortation "beyond the Jordan in the wilderness" (*to the east of the Jordan River*), a statement that suggests the writer is living in the land of Canaan.

 ILLUSTRATION 11A contains *two* depictions of ***Mt. Sinai***.

- The *first* is at the *southern tip of the Sinai Peninsula*.
- The *second* is to the *east of the Jordan River*.

At the summit of both are symbols of a theophany, or God's presence (***cloud and lightning***). Superimposed on both is a symbol of the ***covenant*** God made with the Israelites after they left Egypt. Beneath each is a symbol of the ***Tabernacle***. Around each is a ***circle of small circles*** to depict the concept of God's people living in *community*. Life in God's family is not a private affair. Each person is called to manage God's creation responsibly and to care for, and share with, other members of God's family.

Why *two* symbols of Mt. Sinai? All generations of Israelites were to understand themselves as having taken part in the exodus from Egypt, and as having been present at Mt. Sinai when God made the covenant with them. For them, to remember the past was not merely to *recall* it; it was to celebrate that *they had been present* when God made that covenant. Although Mt. Sinai was located in the southern tip of the Sinai Peninsula, it was also in a real sense present wherever they were. They lived amidst God's awesome presence continually. This understanding of "remembering" persists in the minds and hearts of Jewish people today.

 Deuteronomy's central themes are:

The land

The ***question mark*** above Canaan points to what is at stake throughout Deuteronomy: Israel's claim to the Promised Land. Moses reminds the people that the land remains God's property; God merely grants the Israelites the right to dwell within it as His tenants. The people are not to presume that they will live in the land forever. They will remain in the land only as long as they remain faithful to the covenant God made with them at Mt. Sinai. If they treat the covenant lightly and break it persistently, they will lose the land. Therefore, to ensure that they do not lose the land, the people are urged to avoid every semblance of disobedience, 4:26,27; 11:17; 28:15–68. This exhortation lies at the heart of Deuteronomy.

The Lord alone

The first commandment is of great importance; it is referred to in Deuteronomy 4:15–24; 5:6–10; 6:4–9. God urges the Israelites to shun all false worship, and demands that they destroy all pagans and their shrines to eliminate all temptations to idolatry, 7:16,25,26; 12:1–3; 20:10–18. Severe treatment is to be

meted out to any Israelite who encourages others to worship false gods, and any city that succumbs to pagan worship is to be put under the ban (i.e., excluded from membership in God's community), 13:1–18.

The symbols for **Sinai**, **theophany**, and **covenant** *east of the Jordan River* sum up the urgent tone of Moses' preaching. God's people are always to remember that the awesome presence they first saw at Sinai is a continuing presence. Furthermore, the covenant made at Sinai did not apply merely to the fathers of old, but to every subsequent generation, 5:1–5.

One sanctuary

The Genesis narrative refers to the presence of a number of altars, 12:7,8; 22:9; 26:25; 33:20; 35:1–7. Exodus 20:24 permitted the existence of a number of altars. However, Deuteronomy stresses *one God, one altar!* It rejects the notion of God dwelling materially in any building made by human hands, and insists that only God's *name* dwells in such structures, Deuteronomy 12:5,11,14,18,21,26; 14:23,25; 15:20; 16:2,6,7,11,15,21; 17:8,10. The underlying concern is that it is easier to maintain proper worship practices and loyalty to God when there is only one place of worship, but more difficult when there are many.

Deuteronomy does not specify the name or location of "the place" where the people are to worship God after they enter the land. The concept of "one God—one place" plays an important role in the narrative that unfolds after Israel enters the land.

Blessings and curses

Deuteronomy stresses God's kindness as the motivating factor for Israel's obedience. It goes a step further and insists that obedience is rewarded and disobedience is punished. Those who obey the Lord will be rewarded with a peaceful and untroubled life in the land, abundant fertility, and all things that make life happy and prosperous. The disobedient will receive the reverse of all this and, worse yet, will be driven from the land, 4:26,27. The theme of reward and punishment is set forth in the blessing/curse formula of a Covenant of Human Obligation, 7:12–15; 11:13–32; 27:11–26; c. 28; 29:16–29; 30:1–10, 15–20.

Choose life today

In Deuteronomy, Moses confronts the Israelites with the need to make a decision concerning whether they will be obedient or disobedient, and whether they will obey the God of the exodus or follow other gods. There is no middle ground. The decision is one involving life or death. Deuteronomy goes to great lengths to encourage the people to make a decision for obedience and life, 32:46,47. It appeals passionately to both the community of Israel and the individual Israelite to hear and respond to God's appeal "this day," 4:10–14,39,40; 5:1,2.

To heighten the sense of urgency, the hearer is addressed directly as "you," transported back to the foot of Mt. Sinai to view the awesome presence of God and to hear God's voice from "the fire," and then whisked back to the plains of Moab to hear Moses' solemn admonitions, 26:16–19; 29:10–15.

Deuteronomy in Outline

❶ Introduction to the Deuteronomic Law-Code (1:1–11:32)

General Historical Introduction, 1:1–4:43

- a. Historical survey, 1:1–3:29
- b. The goodness of God's Law, 4:1–40
- c. Cities of refuge, 4:41–43

Detailed Introduction to the Law, 4:44–11:32

- a. The context in which the Law was given, 4:44–49
- b. The giving of the Law at Mt. Sinai, 5:1–33
- c. Guidelines for keeping the first commandment, 6:1–25
- d. Warnings against involvement with foreign nations and gods, 7:1–26
- e. Lessons learned in the wilderness: Trust and obey God! 8:1–20
- f. Lessons learned from the golden calf, 9:1–10:22
- g. Exhortation to take the Sinai Covenant seriously, 11:1–32

❷ The Deuteronomic Law-Code (12:1–26:19)

- a. Worship *one God in one place*, 12:1–31
- b. Warnings against idolatrous practices, 12:32–13:18; 17:2–7; 18:9–14
- c. Food and tithes; 14:1–29
- d. Sabbatical release for the poor, 15:1–18
- e. Sacrifice of the firstborn of flock and herd, 15:19–23
- f. Festivals and feast-days, 16:1–17
- g. Laws governing those holding important offices in Israel, 16:18–18:22
  - Judge, 16:18–20; 17:8–13
  - King, 17:14–20
  - Priest, 18:1–8
  - Prophet, 18:9–22
- h. Cities of refuge, justice, witnesses, 19:1–21
- i. Rules for the conduct of a Holy War, 20:1–20; 21:10–14; 23:9–14
- j. Dealing with murder by an unknown person, 21:1–9
- k. Dealing with social problems, 21:15–22:12
- l. Sex and marriage, 22:13–30
- m. Who may worship the Lord, 23:1–8
- n. Humanitarian and religious obligations, 23:15–25:16
- o. Destroy the despised Amalekites, 25:17–19
- p. Liturgies relating to the offering of first-fruits and tithes, 26:1–15
- q. Final exhortation, 26:16–19

❸ Final Speeches, (27:1–30:20)

- a. Blessings and curses, 27:1–28:68 (28:47–68 relates to the catastrophe of exile)
- b. Warning to people in exile, 29:1–27
- c. Promise of mercy to those in exile, 30:1–20

4 Conclusion to Genesis-Deuteronomy (31:1–34:12)

    a.   Joshua chosen as Moses' successor, 31:1–8,14,15

    b.   A covenant ceremony, to be observed every seven years, is introduced, 31:9–13

    c.   Law tablets placed in the Ark of the Covenant, 31:23–29

    d.   The Song of Moses

        ● Moses commanded to sing, 31:14–22

        ● The song of Moses, 31:30–32:47

    e.   Moses blesses the Israelites, 33:1–29

    f.   Moses ascends Mt. Nebo, sees the Promised Land, dies, and is buried in the land of Moab, 32:48–52, 34:1–12

1 Numbers 10:11–36:13 describes Israel's journey from Sinai to Kadesh-barnea, the sending of the twelve spies, the abortive attempt to capture Canaan, the 38 years at Kadesh-barnea, the journey from Kadesh-barnea to the Transjordan, the conquest of the Moabites and Ammonites, and the assigning of land east of the Jordan River to the tribes of Reuben, Gad, and the half-tribe of Manasseh.

2 Although one might expect Deuteronomy to describe the actual conquest of the Promised Land, it does not do so. Deuteronomy begins by taking the reader back to Mt. Sinai (which it calls Mt. Horeb), and outlines the journey from Sinai to the Transjordan a second time, 1:1–4:40.

3 Although there is considerable overlap between Deuteronomy and the writings that precede it, Deuteronomy does not mesh well with those writings. However, it does serve as a meaningful introduction to what follows in Joshua through 2 Kings. Deuteronomic expressions, themes, and emphases recur throughout these writings, and often constitute the framework for the narrative materials they contain. Deuteronomy's central themes have influenced the contents of Joshua, Judges, Samuel, and Kings. The families of related materials are as follows:

GENESIS through NUMBERS

Creation—Patriarchs—Sinai—Transjordan

DEUTERONOMY through 2 KINGS

Sinai—Transjordan—Conquest—Judges—Monarchy

4 2 Kings 24,25 describe the Babylonian destruction of Judah and Jerusalem in 587 B.C. Although 1 and 2 Chronicles also deal with the biblical narrative, the first ten chapters of 1 Chronicles deal with the history of the world prior to David merely as a list of names from Adam to Saul. *The writer sees Israel's history as beginning with David.* The spirit of Chronicles flows on through Ezra and Nehemiah which deal with the period beyond the return of the exiles from Babylon in 538 B.C. These four writings are referred to as the *Chronicler's History*.

1 Unit 8 pointed out that the covenant God made with Israel at Sinai resembled an ancient Hittite Suzerainty Treaty in structure. Its six parts were:

    a. A **preamble**, in which the king making the treaty identifies himself;

    b. An **historical prologue** listing the king's gracious treatment of the vassal with whom he is making the treaty;

    c. The **stipulations** the vassal is to observe;

    d. The provisions for the **preservation and re-reading** of the treaty;

    e. The list of the gods who are **witnesses** to the treaty;

    f. The **blessings and curses** those who kept or broke the treaty will experience.

2 The same pattern can be found in Deuteronomy 1–30.

    a. God's self-identification; frequent references in chs. 1–3 and elsewhere;

    b. The historical prologue, 1:1–4:43;

    c. The laws binding on Israel—

        ● initial exhortation, 4:44–11:32;

        ● the laws in detail, 12:1–26:19;

    d. Preservation and rereading, 27:8;

    e. Witnesses: Not *other gods*, but *God's creation*—the heavens and the earth;

    f. Blessings and curses, 27:1–28:68.

3 Deuteronomy reads like an aging father's final advice to his children. Its characteristics are obvious and much of its vocabulary is distinctive; these features stand out even in English translations. The book has a warmth, zeal, and urgency of spirit that weaves its way through two foundational truths:

    a. God has been good to Israel. In the mighty event of the Exodus, God rescued Israel from slavery in Egypt, 6:21–23; 11:1–7; 24:18,22; 26:5–9. Israel's great numbers did not move God to do this; the Israel God rescued was the fewest of all peoples, 7:7,8. Furthermore, God did not give Israel the land of Canaan because Israel was righteous and deserved it, but because the Canaanites who lived in it were wicked, 9:4–6. *Grace alone moved God to choose the nation and act on its behalf.*

    b. God earnestly desires Israel to respond to His grace and goodness in willing obedience. The people must remember that God lives in their midst, and that His presence is awesome. The writer repeatedly describes God's presence in terms of fire, 4:10–14,33,36; 5:1–5; 5:22–27. He does more than list laws; he passionately commands Israel to obey them, heaps one motive for obedience on another, and constantly reminds his audience of the consequences of disobedience.

4 Other farewell speeches that occur in the Bible are:

    ● *Jacob*, Genesis 49;

    ● *Joshua*, Joshua 23,24;

    ● *Samuel*, 1 Samuel 12;

    ● *David*, 1 Kings 2:1–9;

    ● *Jesus*, John 13–17.

The Deuteronomic Style

Although Deuteronomy is structured as a speech from beginning to end, it uses vocabulary and phraseology not found in the first four "books of Moses," Genesis through Numbers. The following passages convey the spirit of some of the expressions that occur repeatedly in Deuteronomy 4–11 and are reflected in numerous statements and phrases in Joshua, Judges, Samuel, and Kings.

- *"These are the decrees and the statutes and ordinances"* that God gave to the Israelites, 4:45; 5:1; 6:1; 6:20.

- *"You must observe them diligently,"* 4:5,6; 5:1; 6:3; 7:12; 8:1.

- *"You must study and teach them in the land,"* 5:1; 5:31; 11:19.

- *"You must teach them to your children,"* 4:9,10; 11:19.

- *"…that they may do them in the land that I am giving them to possess,"* 5:31; 6:1,10,18; 9:5.

- *"Obedience will ensure long life and prosperity,"* 4:40; 5:33; 6:2,3; 6:24; 11:9.

- *"You shall love the lord your God,"* 6:5; 10:12; 11:13.

- *"With all your heart, and with all your soul, and with all your might,"* 4:29; 6:5; 10:12; 11:13.

- *"Keep these words that I am commanding you this day in your heart,"* 6:6; 11:18.

- *"Walk in God's ways and fear Him,"* 8:6; 10:20; 11:22.

- *"Do not follow other gods, and do not serve them,"* 6:14; 7:4; 11:16.

- *"If you serve other gods, God's anger will flare up against you,"* 6:15; 7:4; 11:17.

- *"Do not forget the Lord your God,"* 6:12; 8:11.

- *"I am setting before you today a blessing and a curse,"* 11:26; see also 30:19.

- *"The land that God swore to your ancestors,"* 6:10,18,23; 7:13; 10:11.

- *"A land flowing with milk and honey,"* 6:3; 11:9.

- *"Do what is right and good in the sight of the Lord,"* 6:18; see also 12:28 and 13:18.

- *"You shall not turn aside to the right hand or to the left,"* 5:22.

11A The closing chapters of Numbers describe the Israelites destroying several enemy nations in the region to the east of the Jordan River. Although one might expect the next book, Deuteronomy, to describe the people entering the Promised Land, it does not. It depicts Moses speaking earnestly to the Israelites preparing to cross the Jordan River and conquer Canaan.

Throughout Deuteronomy, Moses stresses that the Israelites are not to take for granted that they will possess the Promised Land forever. God, who rescued His people in the Exodus and made a covenant with them at Mt. Sinai, calls them to obedience. If they ignore His call, they will lose both the favor of God and the land they are about to enter. Therefore, the Israelites are to let nothing interfere with their loyalty to God.

The key themes in Deuteronomy are:

- The land that the people are about to enter belongs to God. Whether or not the people remain in the land will depend on whether they obey the stipulations of the Sinai Covenant.
- The people are to worship the Lord alone.
- When they enter the land, the people are to worship the Lord at one central sanctuary.
- If the people render the Lord due honor and obedience, they will be *blessed*. If they do not, they will be *cursed*.
- God's presence at Sinai had been awesome and overwhelming, and that presence continues to live in the midst of Israel. Indeed, the people are to see themselves as living constantly *in the shadow of Sinai*, and are to *choose life* each and every day.

11B
- The first 11 chapters of Deuteronomy contain introductory materials that deal with both historical and legal issues.
- Chs. 12–26 contain what scholars refer to as the Deuteronomic Code. They spell out many details that define obedience to God's laws.
- Deuteronomy's final eight chapters deal with issues relating to blessings and curses, the transfer of authority from Moses to Joshua, and Moses' death.

11C Although there is much historical overlap between Deuteronomy and the four books that precede it (Genesis–Numbers), Deuteronomy meshes well with, and has influenced greatly, the contents of the historical books that follow it (Joshua–2 Kings).

11D The themes of the six-part structure of the covenant God made with the Israelites at Mt. Sinai surface repeatedly within Deuteronomy. The work presents itself as a farewell speech from Moses, who passionately urges the Israelites to take the Sinai covenant seriously. If they do not, they will suffer dire consequences.

11E Deuteronomy contains many words and phrases that are not found in Genesis–Numbers, but are found in the historical writings that follow it (Joshua–2 Kings).

CROSS WAYS

2 SECTION

UNITS 11–20

From the Conquest to the Babylonian Exile

UNIT 12

The Conquest

The Events and Theology of the Conquest of Canaan under Joshua

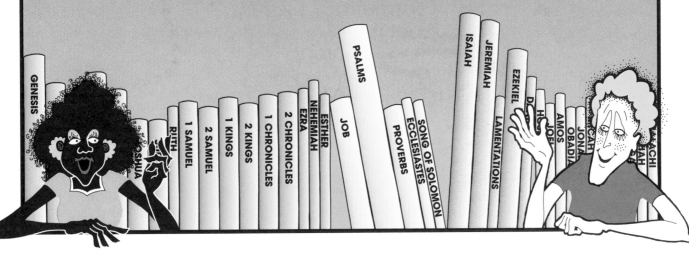

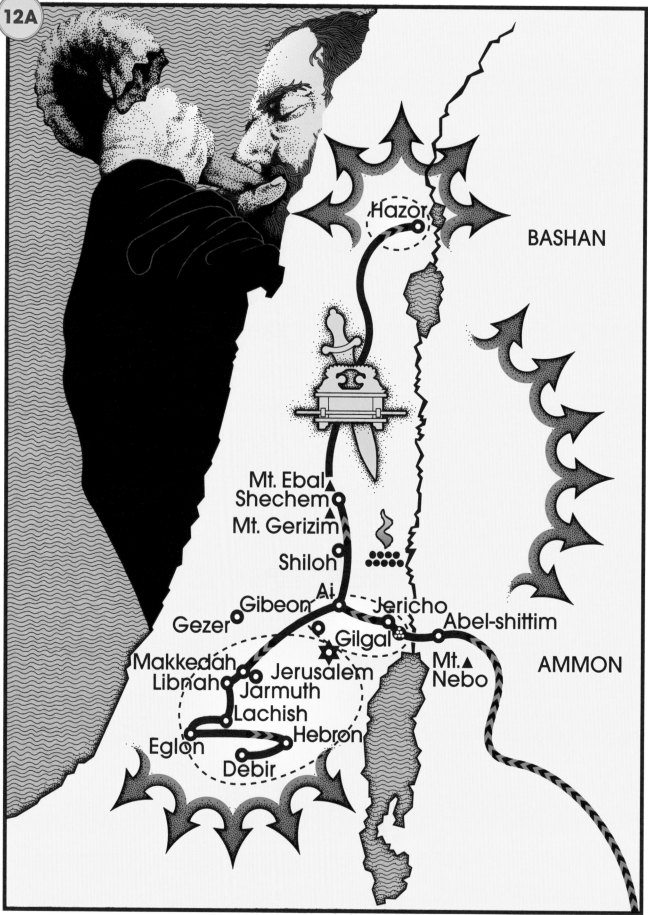

12A

BASHAN

Hazor

Mt. Ebal
Shechem
Mt. Gerizim

Shiloh

Ai

Gibeon

Gezer

Jericho

Gilgal

Abel-shittim

Makkedah
Libnah

Jerusalem

Jarmuth

Lachish

Hebron

Eglon

Debir

Mt.
Nebo

AMMON

In the Hebrew scriptures, Joshua is the first of a series of books referred to as *The Former Prophets*, Joshua through 2 Kings. They are called this because the great men of ancient Israel portrayed in them, who guided the Israelites in their early history, were regarded as divinely inspired persons called to speak and act for God.

The Israelites eventually took possession of the Promised Land under the leadership of Joshua. The contents of the Book of Joshua are more than a narrative about past events. They are also an admonition to future Israelites to continue to cleanse the land of foreign elements and pagan gods.

1 ILLUSTRATION 12A (*top left*) shows **Joshua blowing on a shofar**, a trumpet made from a ram's horn, calling the people to battle.

2 *Semi-circle of arrows in the Transjordan:* The conquest of the region east of the Jordan River (from the territory of **AMMON** to that of Og, king of **BASHAN**) is reported in Numbers 21:21–35 and Deuteronomy 2:26–3:11.

3 After crossing the Jordan River, the Israelites camped at **Gilgal** and then conquered **Jericho** and **Ai**. At **Shechem**, the Israelites and the aliens who had joined their community took part in a covenant ceremony, 8:30–35. A second covenant ceremony at Shechem is reported in ch. 24.

4 After the Israelites made a treaty with the people of **Gibeon** (ch. 9), a coalition of five southern cities (**Jerusalem**, **Hebron**, **Jarmuth**, **Lachish**, and **Eglon**) attacked Gibeon. The Israelites came to the rescue of Gibeon and destroyed the southern coalition (*semi-circle of arrows pointing south*), 10:1–27. The Israelites then conquered other southern cities, including **Makkedah**, **Libnah**, **Gezer**, and **Debir**.

5 Finally, the Israelites conquered an extensive area ruled by Jabin, king of the northern region centered around **Hazor** (*semi-circle of arrows pointing north*). Reference is made to the overthrow of Jabin and the destruction of Hazor in Judges 4.

6 *Ark of the Covenant; sword:* The Israelites viewed the conquest as a Holy War in which God was leading them, and through which God was giving them possession of the land He promised to the patriarchs. The Ark of the Covenant plays an important role in the narrative, particularly in relation to the crossing of the Jordan (ch. 3) and the capture of Jericho, ch. 6.

7 Joshua cast lots at **Shiloh** to determine how some of the land west of the Jordan was to be carved up and allocated to the tribes of Benjamin, Simeon, Zebulun, Issachar, Asher, Naphtali, and Dan, chs. 18,19.

8 *Altar west of the Jordan:* When the East Bank tribes of Reuben, Gad, and the half-tribe of Manasseh returned to their assigned territory east of the Jordan River, they built an altar on the West Bank of the river prior to crossing it. The West Bank tribes became so angry that they decided to annihilate the East Bank tribes. However, the matter was eventually settled amicably, ch. 22.

9 **Mt. Ebal** and **Mt. Gerizim** are mentioned in Joshua 8:30–35. (See also Deuteronomy 11:29 ; 27:4,12,13; Judges 9:7.) They lie to the north and south of Shechem—today's Nablus. Mt. Gerizim eventually became the Samaritans' holy mountain.

In the closing chapters of Deuteronomy, the Israelites are described as a *numerous people*. They are reminded of the significance of the Sinai covenant, profess allegiance to it, and stand poised to cross the Jordan to take possession of the land promised to the patriarchs. Although Moses will die before the conquest takes place, he has already appointed Joshua to be his successor, Deuteronomy 34:9–12. Joshua 5:13–15 describes Joshua experiencing a vision of God's presence similar to that experienced by Moses prior to the Exodus event, Exodus 3:1–6.

The book of Joshua's account of the actual conquest begins in ch. 6. The preceding chapters describe the following preliminary events.

1 God commissions Joshua to take charge of His people and prepare for the crossing of the Jordan and the conquest, 1:1–11.

2 The conquest must be undertaken by a united Israel. Therefore, Joshua commands the men of the tribes that have chosen land east of the Jordan (Reuben, Gad, and the half-tribe of Manasseh) to make arrangements for their wives, children, and cattle to remain secure while they assist with the conquest of Canaan, 1:12–18; see also Numbers 32. Eventually, the East Bank tribes lead the other tribes through the Jordan into the land to do battle against the Canaanites, 4:11–14.

3 Two spies are sent to get information to help develop a strategy to capture Jericho, ch. 2. The spies visit Rahab the harlot, whose home is located in Jericho's casemate walls. Most likely Rahab would have learned much about Jericho's defense system from her clientele—which would have included military personnel. The mission of the spies seems a little strange in light of the eventual miraculous capture of Jericho. Possibly the purpose of the story is to explain why the family of Rahab was not destroyed but allowed to continue living in the land. (Rahab was an ancestor of King David, Matthew 1:5.)

4 Ch. 3 describes the Israelites crossing the Jordan River. The narrative states that when the feet of those carrying the Ark of the Covenant touch the edge of the Jordan, the waters stop flowing and separate to permit the Israelites to pass through. God's power and presence, symbolized by the Ark of the Covenant, make possible the people's entry into the land. When all the Israelites reach the West Bank of the Jordan River, the priests carrying the Ark of the Covenant also enter, and the Jordan's water resumes its flow.

5 Stone memorials are erected to help Israel remember the crossing; one at Gilgal (4:1–8), and apparently another in the middle of the Jordan 4:9,10. These memorials are to remind present and future generations that the God who opened the waters to rescue the Israelites from Egypt also opened the waters of the Jordan River to enable them to enter the Promised Land, 4:19–24.

6 The impending invasion strikes terror into the hearts of the Canaanites, 5:1.

7 Joshua 5:2–9 reports a puzzling event. All the men who left Egypt in the Exodus would not enter the Promised Land—they had not "listened to the voice of the Lord" in relation to the report that Joshua and Caleb gave after secretly surveying the land from Kadesh-barnea, Numbers 13,14. Although those men had been circumcised, none of the male children born during the wilderness wanderings had been circumcised, Joshua 5:5. One wonders why Moses did not attend to this matter. However, for the present generation of males to be identified as true Israelites, they had to circumcised. So Joshua deals with the situation at Gibeath-haaraloth ("Hill of the Foreskins").

8 Israel camps at Gilgal and celebrates the Passover. *The manna ceases*, and the people eat the produce of Canaan, 5:10–12. In eating food grown in the land, the Israelites anticipate their eventual possession of Canaan and the bounty they will enjoy within its borders.

During the period between the Old and New Testaments, the hope developed that when the messianic age came, the manna would fall again.

> *And it will happen at that time that the treasury of manna will come down again from on high, and they will eat of it those years because these are they who will have arrived at the consummation of time.* (2 Baruch 29:8; see also John 6.)

9 The Lord declares Himself to be the actual Commander-in-Chief of the armies of Israel, and Joshua to be His visible representative, 5:13–15. Throughout the narrative, Joshua is presented as an exemplary leader who renders the Lord total obedience.

The Conquest Campaigns

Joshua 6–11 describe how Canaan fell into Israel's hands as a result of three swift campaigns. Although Judges 1:1–2:10 contains information about Israel's military ventures within Canaan, it emphasizes that the Israelites failed to eliminate the Canaanites from the land. This unit will examine the Joshua account.

 The First Campaign (Joshua 6–8)

- After crossing the Jordan, Israel established a foothold on the west bank of the Jordan and set up camp at **Gilgal**.

- **Jericho** was put under siege and captured in a miraculous manner, Joshua 6. The real point of the story is that the Lord fought for Israel, and Joshua and the people obeyed the laws of Holy War, 6:15–21,24. (See also Deuteronomy 20.)

- Israel's armies then moved up into the hill country and attempted to capture Ai. Although those sent to spy in the city boasted that victory was certain, the Israelites were defeated, 7:1–5.

  There were reasons for the defeat. First, the Israelites did not consult the Lord prior to undertaking the campaign; they drew up their own strategy, 7:2,3. Second, Achan had broken the rules of Holy War in relation to the capture of Jericho by keeping part of the booty taken there. Because one of their number had broken the ban in relation to keeping booty, the Israelites themselves were now under the ban and the success of the conquest was in jeopardy. Because the evil done by the head of a clan tainted the clan as a whole, the Israelites destroyed Achan, his family and clan, and their possessions, 7:6–26.

  God then issued instructions concerning how **Ai** was to be captured. Joshua and the people obeyed, and the campaign proved successful, 8:1–29. The rules of Holy War were observed, and all living in Ai were killed.

- Next follows a section which seems to interrupt the flow of the conquest narrative, Joshua 8:30–35. The Israelites go north to Shechem, Joshua builds an altar on **Mt. Ebal** to the *north* of the city, and then leads a covenant ratification ceremony. (Deuteronomy 27:4,5 says Moses commanded Joshua to build an altar in the land and set up large stones on which a copy of the law would be written.) Joshua 8:33 states that, during the ceremony, priests stood in front of both Mt. Ebal and **Mt. Gerizim** (to the *south* of Shechem).

 The Second Campaign (Joshua 9–10)

- Israel moved down into the southern hill country of Canaan, bypassing the fortress city of Jerusalem in the process. The invaders were tricked into making a treaty with four southern cities (**Gibeon**, *Chephirah, Beeroth, Kiriath-jearim*), the chief of which was Gibeon. The Gibeonites' goal was to escape the fate of Jericho and Ai. Once again in this event, the Israelites took action without consulting the Lord—and found themselves compromised as a result, 9:3–27.

- The Gibeonites' action aroused the ire of five Canaanite kings from **Jerusalem**, **Hebron**, **Jarmuth**, **Lachish**, and **Eglon**, who formed a coalition and made reprisal attacks against the Gibeonites. The Israelites honored the treaty with the Gibeonites, went to their aid, subdued their oppressors, and killed the five kings who were hiding in a cave at Makkedah, 10:1–27.

- This victory achieved, the Israelites moved on to further conquests and captured the city-states of **Makkedah**, **Libnah**, **Lachish**, **Gezer**, **Eglon**, **Hebron**, and **Debir**, 10:28–43. No mention is made of Israel capturing **Jerusalem** at this time. (Judges 1:8 says the people of Judah captured and destroyed Jerusalem. Judges 1:21 says the Benjaminites captured Jerusalem and shared it with the Jebusites. According to 2 Samuel 5:6–10, David captured

Jerusalem and made it his capital.) **Gilgal** seems to have served as a military base during the first two campaigns.

● The report of the capture of southern Canaan contains obvious Holy War elements:

> The enemy feared Israel, 10:2;
>
> The Lord fought for Israel, 10:14;
>
> Hailstones from the sky killed the enemy, 10:11;
>
> The Lord prolonged daylight to enable the Israelites to achieve total victory, 10:12–14;
>
> No survivors were left, 10:28,30,33,37,39,40;
>
> The enemy's horses were hamstrung, and their chariots incinerated, 11:9.

3 The Third Campaign (Joshua 11)

● In the third campaign, Israel's armies marched north and eventually won a decisive victory at **Hazor** against a large northern coalition. The coalition consisted of King Jabin of Hazor; the kings of Shimron and Achshaph; those who ruled the Arabah, the lowland, Naphath-dor, the Canaanites to the east and west, the Amorites, the Hittites, the Perizzites, the Jebusites, and the Hivites. Although the account is brief, we are told that Joshua did everything in obedience to the Lord (11:15), that all enemies were exterminated (11:20), and that the conquest was total, 11:23.

● *Ch. 12 contains a summary of Israel's victories.* The conquest of the Transjordan is described in 12:1–6. The conquest of the west bank regions is summarized in 12:7–24; this section refers to many places not mentioned elsewhere. The conquest was now complete. The land was in the hands of the Israelites. Or was it?

ANOTHER VIEW OF THE CONQUEST

1

According to the accounts outlined above, Joshua was the leader of a united Israel. He planned and led three lightning attacks into the center, the southern, and the northern areas of Canaan—thus enabling the Israelites to take complete possession of the land. The campaign was a violent one. Cities were razed. The native Canaanite population was all but exterminated. The Israelites swept everything away as they advanced. Joshua 10:40–42 and 11:16–23 suggest that the conquest was thorough and complete.

2

However, there are hints within the book itself that the whole procedure was not as simple, and the sweep not as clean, as suggested, 13:1,2,13; 23:1–13. Indications are that much more needed to be done before the Israelites could claim that "the land had rest from war," 11:23. Several passages (15:63; 16:10; 17:12,18) state that the Israelites were unable to expel the Canaanites from a number of places. According to Judges 1:1, after Joshua dies the people ask, "Who shall go up first for us against the Canaanites, to fight against them?"

3

Even more significant is the account of the conquest recorded in Judges 1:1–3:6. It will be studied in Unit 13. Joshua 18:2–10 gives the impression that the conquest was carried out along the lines suggested in Judges 1:1–3:6.

1 The division of the land is outlined in Joshua 13:1–21:45. Although Joshua 11:23 states that the conquest was complete, 13:1–6 indicates that it was anything but complete. Even so, the Lord commanded Joshua to divide the land among the tribes, 13:7.

2 Joshua 13–21 describe the division of the land among the tribes. The factor of tribal size played a role in determining how much territory each tribe was to receive. Joshua 18:1–10 and 19:51 state that some of the allocations were made at a meeting at Shiloh (where the Tent of Meeting—not the Tabernacle—was located).

- Manasseh (half-tribe), Gad and Reuben, Joshua 13:8–14:5
- Hebron is assigned to Caleb, 14:6–15
- Judah, ch. 15
- The Joseph tribes (including the half-tribe of Manasseh), 16:1–17:18
- Benjamin, 18:11–18
- Simeon, 19:1–9
- Zebulun, 19:10–16
- Issachar, 19:17–23
- Asher, 19:24–31
- Naphtali, 19:32–39
- Dan, 19:40–48
- Joshua is given the city of Timnath-serah in Ephraim, 19:49,50

ADDITIONAL COMMENTS

1 Cities of refuge are established—three to the east (Bezer, Ramoth, Golan) and three to the west (Kadesh, Shechem, Kiriath-arba) of the Jordan River, ch. 20.

2 The Levites are allocated *cities*, not *territory*, ch. 21.

3 The tribes assigned land on the East Bank of the Jordan return home, 22:1–10. However, a misunderstanding arises over an altar they build, 22:11–34. Peace is restored when the returning tribes assure the west bank tribes that the altar was to serve as a witness and would not be used for sacrifice. Eventually, the issue of centralization of worship becomes a very important factor in the life of the Israelites. As Unit 11 pointed out, Deuteronomy insists that Israel's one God must be worshiped in one place, Deuteronomy 12:5,11,14,18,21,26.

4 In Joshua 23, Joshua makes a farewell speech in which he sets forth the conditions under which the Israelites' life in the land will be blessed. Joshua exhorts the people to worship only the God of Israel. Although some nations remain in the land, the Lord will drive them out if the Israelites do not worship the gods of these nations. If the Israelites do not worship the Lord, and the Lord alone, they will lose the Promised Land. The speech hints at future challenges and problems.

5 The final chapter of Joshua describes a covenant ceremony at Shechem (24:1–28), Joshua's death (24:29,30), the interment of Joseph's bones at Shechem (24:32), and the death and burial of Eleazar, Aaron's son, 24:33.

1 Joshua 24:1–28 describes the events of an important ceremony at **Shechem**, a town strategically located in the narrow pass between **Mt. Gerizim** and **Mt. Ebal**. Excavations at Shechem indicate that it was an important religious center before the arrival of the Israelites. The Old Testament text indicates that, after the conquest, Israel used the locality in its own worship life. It was still an important center at the time of Jesus, John 4. (Gerizim can be equated with Shechem.)

2 The ceremony that took place at Shechem contains some elements of a covenant renewal ceremony.

 a. The first part of 24:2 contains a *preamble*.

 b. Then comes an *historical prologue*, 24:2–13. Joshua outlines the nation's history to the assembly, tracing it from the period of the patriarchs through the Exodus and the wilderness period to the time of the conquest.

 c. Joshua then confronts the people with a *challenging question*. Will they serve the Lord or will they serve the gods their fathers had served back in Mesopotamia—which the Canaanites around them were still serving, 24:14–28? Joshua exhorts the people to remember that the Lord is a jealous God—a God who will tolerate no rivals.

 d. The people respond by *declaring their desire to serve the Lord* who had brought them out of Egypt and led them into Canaan. Joshua then commands them to put away their false gods. The ceremony is brought to a close with the renewal of the covenant.

 e. In 24:22, the people declare themselves to be *witnesses* to the covenant procedures. In 24:26–27, Joshua writes the covenant's statutes and ordinances in a book, and sets up a large stone as a witness to the covenant renewal ceremony just completed.

3 In the covenant ceremony, the Lord stresses that the people are to put away all foreign gods. If they do, they will be *blessed*; if they do not, they will be *cursed*. The narrative that follows in Judges through 2 Kings reveals that because the Israelites failed to take the covenant seriously, they made their destruction inevitable.

THE INTERNATIONAL SCENE

1 The land in which Joshua's campaigns took place was situated among a number of world powers. Canaan came under the domination of whatever power was in control of that part of the world at that time. One would then expect that the greatest obstacle to the Israelite invaders would not have been the Canaanite forces but the imperial powers of Mesopotamia.

2 At the time of Joshua's invasion, although Egypt was the nominal overlord of Canaan, it was unable to exercise effective control over this region. Furthermore, the Hittite and Mesopotamian powers were either plagued with internal troubles or were in no position to police Canaan.

3 At the time of the Israelite invasion and for some time afterward, Canaan was a political power vacuum. From a *human* point of view, this made the Israelite invasion of Canaan possible. From a *theological* point of view, God can use all aspects of history to accomplish His purposes.

12A The goal of Joshua is not merely to describe the conquest, but to proclaim to the Israelites the dramatic story of the *Lord's* victory through Joshua. The book sets out to inscribe on the people's memory the fact that their victories were won, not by their military power, but by the *Lord* who brought them into the land, led them in their military struggles, and overcame their opponents.

12B Prior to undertaking the conquest, the Israelites:

- Make arrangements to ensure the safety of the women and children of the tribes who will eventually settle in the territory to the east of the Jordan River;
- Send spies to survey the land and the city of Jericho;
- Pass through the waters of the Jordan River, which stop flowing and wall up to permit the Israelites to enter the Promised Land in a liturgical procession led by Levitical priests carrying the Ark of the Covenant;
- Erect memorial stones to serve as an enduring reminder of their entry into the land;
- Circumcise all males born after the Exodus from Egypt and celebrate a special Passover event at Gilgal on the West Bank of the Jordan River.

12C After the Israelites cross the Jordan, Joshua carries out several military campaigns in Canaan:

- In the *first*, he gains control of Canaan's central region, chs. 6–8;
- In the *second*, he conquers the land's southern region, chs. 9–10;
- In the *third*, the Israelites capture the northern section of Canaan, ch. 11.

The land is then divided among the tribes.

Although some passages in Joshua suggest that the conquest was swift and complete, other passages (e.g., 18:2–10; see also Judges 1:1–3:6) suggest that the Israelites were unable to expel the Canaanites from a number of regions.

12D Joshua 13–21 reports how the land was divided among the tribes.

Six cities of refuge were established—three on each side of the Jordan River. The Levites (the priestly tribe) were allocated cities—not territory.

12E Just as Moses, prior to his death, had exhorted the Israelites to remain true to the covenant God had made with them at Sinai, Joshua 24:1–28 describes Moses' successor, Joshua, doing the same during a covenant ceremony at Shechem—located between Mts. Ebal and Gerizim. This final chapter also describes the death and burial of Joshua and Eleazar, and the interment of Joseph's bones at Shechem.

While the conquest was being carried out, major powers to the north and south of the Promised Land were preoccupied with internal troubles—which made it impossible for them to police what was taking place in Canaan.

CROSS WAYS

2 SECTION

UNITS 11–20

From the Conquest to the Babylonian Exile

UNIT 13

The Judges

The Events and Tensions of the Period of the Judges

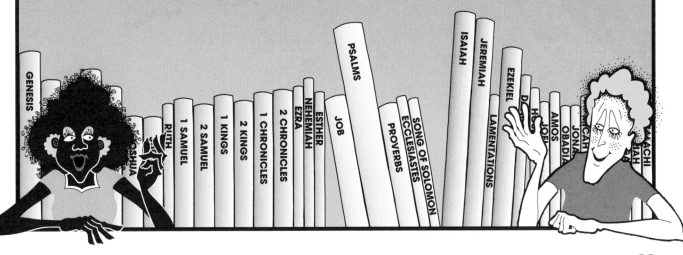

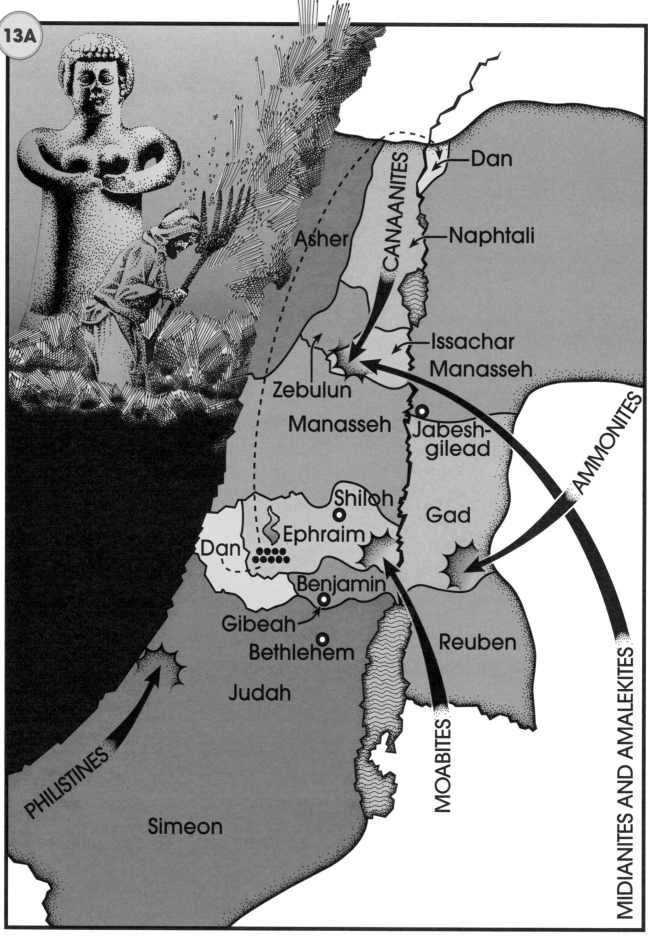

Dan

CANAANITES

Naphtali

Asher

Issachar

Manasseh

Zebulun

Manasseh

Jabesh-
gilead

AMMONITES

Shiloh

Gad

Ephraim

Dan

Benjamin

Reuben

Gibeah

Bethlehem

Judah

MOABITES

PHILISTINES

Simeon

MIDIANITES AND AMALEKITES

ILLUSTRATION 13A depicts:

- The *territory allotted to each of the twelve tribes*;
- The worship of *fertility gods* which many Israelites practiced. (Judges 3:5,6 states that Israelite men married Canaanite women and worshiped their gods);
- Some of the *attacks by other nations* that the Israelites had to deal with.

Although Joshua 11:23 states that the Israelites had captured the entire Promised Land and were enjoying "rest from war," Joshua 13–24 and Judges suggest that many trouble spots remained. Judges describes the Israelites' continuing encounters with the Canaanites within their borders and with other nations beyond their borders.

1 The division of the land allocated to the East Bank tribes (*Reuben*, *Gad*, and the half-tribe of *Manasseh*) is reported in Deuteronomy 3:12–17 and Joshua 13:8–13,15–33. Joshua 14:1–5 speaks of Joshua dividing the territory to the west of the Jordan River bank among the other 9½ tribes. Caleb is given possession of Hebron, Joshua 14:6–15. Territory is assigned to *Judah* in Joshua 15 and to the Joseph tribes (the other half-tribe of *Manasseh* and *Ephraim*) in Joshua 16. Joshua 18:1–10 refers to Joshua (in the vicinity of the Tent of Meeting at *Shiloh*) casting lots to determine what areas the remaining seven tribes should receive. Tribal size played a part in the decision process, Numbers 26:51–56, 33:54–56.

2 Although Judges does not mention *Issachar*, it seems to suggest that each of the other tribes undertook to capture the region allotted to it on an individual basis. However, none of the tribes succeeded in completely removing the Canaanites from the assigned territory. The following passages describe the various campaigns:

    a. *Judah* and *Simeon*, 1:3–20;

    b. *Benjamin*, 1:21;

    c. The Joseph tribes, *Manasseh* and *Ephraim*, 1:22–29;

    d. *Zebulun*, 1:30;

    e. *Asher*, 1:31;

    f. *Naphtali*, 1:33;

    g. *Dan*, 1:34–36.

3 Judges tells of continuing counter-attacks against the Israelites by:

    a. *MOABITES*, 3:12–30;

    b. The unsubdued *CANAANITES*, chs. 4–5;

    c. *MIDIANITES*, chs. 6–8;

    d. *AMMONITES*, chs. 10–11;

    e. *PHILISTINES*, chs. 13–16.

4 Judges 17,18 describe how the *Dan*ites abandoned the territory initially allotted to them, and settled in a region to the north of the Sea of Galilee. When doing this, they took with them a Levite from Bethlehem who had entered the service of Micah (an Ephraimite), and an idol that Micah had installed in a shrine (*altar, flame*) he had built. The suggestion seems to be that the Danites placed the idol in a shrine in their new territory—and installed Jonathan (a grandson of Moses) and his sons to serve as priests.

Judges 1:1–3:6 raises a number of interesting questions and sets the stage for events that follow.

1 Joshua 24:29,30 and Judges 1:1 refer to Joshua's death. Judges 2:6–10 appears to be a ***second*** account of Joshua's death and burial. Some suggest that Judges 1:1–2:10 describes the acquisition of Canaan by the Israelites as a combination of both conquest and gradual infiltration.

2 In Judges 1:2–7, Judah and Simeon join forces to gain control of the territory allotted to them. In doing so, they mete out harsh treatment to Adonibezek, king of Bezek; they cut off his thumbs and big toes, making it impossible for him to wield weapons or to run.

3 Joshua 15:63 suggests that the territory of Judah was assigned to the people of Judah—but because the people of Judah could not drive out Jebusites who lived in Jerusalem, the people of Judah shared the city with them. Joshua 18:28 says that Jerusalem was among the cities allotted to the Benjaminites. Judges 1:8 says that the men of Judah captured and destroyed Jerusalem. Judges 1:21 says that the Benjaminites shared possession of it with the Jebusites who lived there.

4 According to Judges 2:1–5, because the Israelites did not destroy the Canaanites and their religious practices, God permitted the Canaanites remaining in the land to become a snare to the Israelites. Judges 2:11–15 describes the Israelites involving themselves with the Canaanites. Judges 2:16–23 describes the consequences.

5 Judges 3:1–6 contains two interesting thoughts.
- *First*, the writer states that God permitted the Canaanites to remain in the land so that the Israelites might gain experience in war; 3:1,2.
- *Second*, the writer lists the names of those groups that would continue to live in the midst of Israel; 3:3,4.

1 How did the Israelites cope with the threats outlined in 13B? They met them under the charismatic leadership of *judges*. The term "judge" creates the image of a courtroom where a solemn person in a black robe presides over a legal case. The term used in the Book of Judges means something quite different. It refers to military heroes and national saviors—people of power and authority raised up by God to deliver the Israelites in times of crisis.

2 The book indicates that four of the judges were chosen through an act of divine intervention: "the spirit of the Lord came upon him" (*Othniel*, 3:10; *Gideon*, 6:34; *Jephthah*, 11:29; *Samson*, 14:19). The desired outcome of this event was to equip those chosen in this manner to serve as effective leaders to deliver the Israelites from oppression.

3 The judges developed no dynastic system. Little is said about what they did when they were not delivering their people. Possibly they acted as local leaders and helped settle disputes. Possibly there were other judges whose names are not given in the book. The following tabulation sets out the chronology of the period according to the Book of Judges.

OPPRESSOR	YEARS OF OPPRESSION	JUDGE	FROM THE TRIBE	YEARS OF RULE
Cushan-rishathaim	8	**Othniel**	Judah	40
Moabites	18	**Ehud**	Benjamin	80
Philistines	?	Shamgar	?	?
Jabin (Canaanite)	18	**Deborah** and Barak	Ephraim Naphtali	40
Midianites	7	**Gideon**	Manasseh	40
		Tola	Issachar-Ephraim	23
		Jair	Manasseh	22
Ammonites	18	**Jephthah**	Gilead to the east of the Jordan River, possibly with links to Gad	6
		Ibzan	Judah	7
		Elon	Zebulon	10
		Abdon	Ephraim	8
Philistines	40	**Samson**	Dan	20

The six names in **bold** are referred to as "major judges;" the other names as "minor judges."

To the above list might be added the name of Abimelech, the half-Canaanite son of Gideon and self-proclaimed king, whose influence extended over a period of three years; see Judges 9. The name Abimelech means "my father is king," and possibly reflects his desire to be made king.

A note of caution about chronology: Attempts to determine the total period of years Israel was ruled by judges using the numbers under **YEARS OF RULE** above can be futile. Possibly some of the judges did their work in different parts of the land at the same time. Furthermore, the manner in which the Old Testament uses numbers is at times complex and unorthodox. Numbers such as 20, 40, and 80 occur in the above table (and elsewhere in the Old Testament) with sufficient frequency to give rise to questions about their precise significance.

1 The story of each of the major judges is set into a framework that reflects Deuteronomy's view of history. This framework relates Israel's national fortunes to the people's faithfulness, or lack of faithfulness, to the Sinai Covenant. It is summarized in Judges 2:11–19, and repeated again in 3:12–14, 4:1–3, 6:1–2. Its structure is as follows (**A**, **B**, **C**, **D**):

- ● *Apostasy:* Israel sins.
- ● *Battering:* God uses neighboring nations to punish His people.
- ● *Cry:* Israel cries to the Lord for help.
- ● *Deliverance:* The Lord raises up a judge to deliver His people.

2 In the biblical text, the framework reads as follows:

- ● *The people of Israel did what was evil in the sight of the Lord by* _____ (sin specified).
- ● *The Lord gave them over to* _____ (name of oppressor) *who oppressed them for* _____ *years.*
- ● *When the Israelites cried to the Lord for help, the Lord raised up* _____ (name of judge) *to deliver them.*
- ● The story of the judge is then recounted, and the section is closed with, *The land enjoyed peace for* _____ *years.*

Judges 3–16

1 In the *first episode* (3:7–11) the enemy is Cushan-rishathaim; his name is unknown apart from its mention here. The region he ruled is not known. The reason the Lord permitted him to harass Israel was the latter's involvement in Baal worship, 3:7. The name **Othniel** is mentioned also in Joshua 15:16–19, but apart from that reference, and the reference in Judges, nothing is known about him. In Judges 3:10, we read that "the spirit of the Lord came upon him."

2 The *second episode* (3:12–30) tells the story of **Ehud** who delivered the Israelites from oppression by Eglon and the Moabites. Apparently the enemy had crossed the Jordan and taken possession of the "city of palms" (Jericho, perhaps) in Israelite territory. Ehud dispatched the oppressor in the vicinity of Gilgal, a few miles west of the Jordan, and with Ephraimite assistance pushed the Moabites back over the Jordan.

The story contains elements of Middle Eastern humor. Because Ehud was left-handed, his sword would have been strapped to his right leg. However, because Eglon's guards would have assumed that Ehud was right-handed, they would have inspected his left leg rather than his right. Furthermore, the left hand was used to do "unmentionable acts" involving personal hygiene. The fact that Ehud would have used his left hand to hold the sword he used to kill Eglon says something about how the writer viewed Eglon. Furthermore, Eglon is depicted as being so fat that Ehud's sword disappears when he strikes him in the belly. And finally, Eglon's servants think that their king is simply taking a long time in the bathroom when in reality he is dead.

3 The *third episode* (3:31) reports the work of **Shamgar**, who dispatched six hundred Philistines with an ox-goad. The usual framework (*A*, *B*, *C*, *D*) is missing from this one-verse narrative.

4 The *fourth incident* describes the campaigns of **Deborah** and her general, **Barak**, against the northern Canaanites. The story is given in two versions, the first in *prose* (ch. 4) and the second in *poetry* (ch. 5). In the battle fought at Taanach near Megiddo, a tremendous rainstorm turned the brook Kishon into a raging torrent. The chariots of the Canaanites sank into the mud, enabling the forces of Deborah and Barak—who were on higher ground—to gain the upper hand. Sisera's forces were annihilated. He himself fled, but suffered a degrading death at the hand of a woman, Jael the Kenite. In the poetic account of the campaign, mocking reference is made to Sisera's mother waiting in vain for her son to return, 5:28–31. Deborah bemoans the fact that not all the tribes came to help against the Canaanites, 5:15–17.

5 The *fifth episode* (6:1–8:35) describes the campaigns of **Gideon**. The enemies are the Midianites with help from the Amalekites and "the people of the East," 6:3. Just as the Hebrews had swarmed into the land held by the Canaanites, so also the Midianites, Amalekites, and others from the East threatened to overrun Hebrew territory. According to Judges, this took place because the Israelites had been worshiping Amorite gods, 6:10. (*Amorite* is the term Deuteronomy uses for *Canaanite*.)

Ch. 6 explains how the name "The Lord is peace" was given to a place called Ophrah, and how the names Jerubbaal ("Baal fights") and Gideon ("the Smiter") were given to the same man. Gideon's annihilation of the Midianites is described in vivid terms. The Israelite army was reduced from 32,000 to 300 to emphasize that victory came from the Lord and not from Israel's military might. Gideon's disputes with the Ephraimites, and later with the citizens of Succoth and Penuel, point to the importance of the Israelites working in unity.

The people were so impressed with Gideon's leadership abilities that they suggested he be declared

king of Israel, and that a Gideon dynasty be established, 8:22–23. Unfortunately Gideon himself contributed toward Israel's continuing apostasy by making an image, which the people worshiped, 8:27. The Gideon account bristles with difficulties.

An additional incident involving **Abimelech**, a son of Gideon's concubine, is described in 8:29–9:57. Judges 9 describes how Abimelech made it clear that, although his father was unwilling to be declared king of Israel, he himself was a willing candidate for the position. He murdered his brothers (with the exception of Jotham) and had himself proclaimed king at Shechem. Jotham was anything but an enthusiastic supporter of his brother's ambitions. He expressed his feelings in a parable about a bramble, 9:7–21. Abimelech's rule lasted for three years. When some of the people of Shechem contested his rule, Abimelech razed the city and killed its citizens. While Abimelech was trying to conquer the neighboring city of Thebez, a woman threw down from a tower a millstone which crushed his skull. Because it was considered a disgrace to be killed by a woman, Abimelech, with his dying breath, commanded his armor-bearer to kill him with his sword.

The narrative makes a number of theological points: Abimelech was not appointed leader by the Lord. The people of Shechem did not consult the Lord in accepting the leadership of Abimelech. Both suffered for their disregard of the will of the Lord: the Shechemites and their city were destroyed, and Abimelech was killed.

Abimelech's attempt to establish a dynasty ended in a way very similar to that of Saul, 1 Samuel 31. Both of these failed attempts set the stage for the arrival of the one who would eventually establish an acceptable, legitimate dynasty—David!

 In the *sixth* and *seventh episodes*, the work of **Tola** (10:1,2) and **Jair** (10:3–5) is listed. No reference is made to enemies or battles.

 The *eighth episode* describes struggles with the Ammonites and Moabites, 10:6–12:7. The central figure in this narrative is **Jephthah**, an illegitimate son born to Gilead by a prostitute. When Gilead's legitimate sons sent Jephthah away, Jephthah gathered around himself a group of outlaws and carried out raids.

Eventually the elders of Gilead appointed Jephthah to lead the people in battle against the Ammonites and Moabites. In initial negotiations with the Ammonites, Jephthah argued for Israel's right to the land as a gift from God, 11:12–27. The Ammonites did not accept Jephthah's argument, and war resulted, 11:28–33. To ensure the Lord's support, Jephthah promised to sacrifice whatever living thing first came out of his house to greet him when he returned victorious from his campaigns. Most likely, he expected to see an *animal* emerge from the house—since many houses consisted of only one room, with a stable immediately inside the front entrance. Unfortunately for Jephthah, his *daughter* (and only child) came out of the house to greet him. The concluding note in ch. 11 suggests that the incident gave rise to the custom of bewailing virginity among the Israelites. The closing portion of the Jephthah cycle speaks of conflicts among some of the tribes, specifically Gilead and Ephraim, and of differences in dialects among the various groups, 12:1–6. Jephthah is called "judge" only in 12:7.

 The *ninth*, *tenth*, and *eleventh episodes* (12:8–15) are mentioned between the end of the Jephthah cycle and the Samson stories. They refer to **Ibzan**, **Elon**, and **Abdon**. No reference is made to the social or political situation in Israel in relation to these names. If these three judges are listed as numbers *nine*, *ten* and *eleven*, the Samson cycle constitutes episode twelve, Judges 13–16.

 In the *twelfth episode* (Judges 13–16), **Samson** appears and the conflict with the Philistines is introduced. Samson operated as a one-man army. His birth had a miraculous quality, 13:2–14.

His mother was told that her son was to be raised as a Nazirite (Numbers 6:1–21) and was to live under a vow of consecration. Samson's special gift was his incredible strength, the secret of which lay in his Nazirite relationship with the Lord. Judges tells Samson's story with power and color. His marriage with Delilah, a Philistine, was apparently one in which the wife remained with her parents, and the husband paid her periodic visits. No reference is made to open warfare between the Philistines and Hebrews. Samson's encounters with the enemy amounted to skirmishes rather than battles. The Hebrews and Philistines seem to have been able to speak to one another without difficulty; apparently no language problem existed. Samson was a Danite; **ILLUSTRATION 13A** shows the proximity of Dan to Philistine territory.

THE SAMSON NARRATIVE

Some theological observations

Some Nazirites were Nazirites for life, others took only temporary vows. Samson was a Nazirite for life. Nazirites were to abstain from wine and strong drink. They were not to cut their hair. The offering of hair was an offering of one's life, for hair was associated with the life of a person. They could not have contact with a dead body. Contact with the dead rendered the priestly community ritually unclean. Samson was not faithful to his vows. He had contact with a dead animal, and even ate meat from it. He was indirectly responsible for having his hair cut by Delilah, for he told her the secret of his strength—his long hair. Although the narrative does not say that Samson drank wine, it states that he hosted a drinking party.

The Lord was responsible for Samson's birth; Samson was to be the Lord's instrument for dealing with the Philistines. Even Samson's desire to marry a Philistine woman is said to have been a divinely inspired means by which to create an opportunity to harass the Philistines, 14:4; see also 16:1. The Lord gave Samson strength to battle the enemy. The Lord responded to Samson's prayers for water and vengeance, 15:18, 16:28. Ironically, Samson's downfall was brought about by his inability to say "No!" to a woman. (Units 15 and 16 will point out that David and Solomon seemed to have similar problems.) At the same time, Samson's defeat became an opportunity for the Israelites to gain victory over the Philistines.

Judges concludes with events and conditions of the period.

The origin of the shrine at Dan (Judges 17,18)

A certain Micah of Ephraim stole eleven hundred pieces of silver from his mother, but eventually saw fit to return them to her. Although she consecrated all the returned money to the Lord, she used part of it to build a shrine and some images. Micah installed one of his sons as priest and later obtained the services of a Levite from Bethlehem. When the tribe of Dan found itself being harassed by the Philistines to the south, it sent a party of five to examine the territory north of the Sea of Galilee. These five spies visited the shrine in Ephraim and sought God's blessing on their travels (Deuteronomy 20:1–4). Upon their return to their home territory, the spies gave a glowing report—with the result that a large group of Danites ventured out to settle in the new region. They visited the home of Micah of Ephraim along the way and took with them his images and his Levite priest, using them to establish a shrine in their new northern home. The Levite is depicted as one willing to serve the highest bidder. Judges 18:30,31 says that the Danites installed some of Moses' descendants to serve as their priests.

The story has connections with the preceding Samson narrative and with later narratives in Kings. Samson, a Danite, fought the Philistines but the latter seemed to retain the upper hand; hence the desire of the Danites to put distance between themselves and the Philistines. After Solomon's death, the kingdom split. Jeroboam I, the first king of Israel, built shrines at Bethel and Dan—an act that 1 Kings 12:29,30 views as an abomination. The Judges' narrative paints the origin of the shrine at Dan in the darkest of colors!

Wives for the Benjaminites (Judges 19–21)

The men of *Gibeah* in Benjamin sought to abuse a Levite sexually, but after being denied the opportunity to do so they ravished and killed his concubine. The Levite summoned the other tribes of Israel to avenge the crime, which they managed to do after suffering two initial defeats. The six hundred male Benjaminites who survived lacked wives. The other tribes had sworn not to share their women with the Benjaminites, but shuddered at the thought of a tribe in Israel dying out. They therefore devastated the northern Israelite city of *Jabesh-gilead* which had not joined in the campaign against the Benjaminites, preserving only four hundred young virgins who were then given to the Benjaminites as wives. They instructed the two hundred men still lacking wives to take them forcibly from among the young women taking part in a festival at *Shiloh*.

How does this narrative help us understand later narratives? There came the day when Saul, who lived in Gibeah, mustered Israel's armies in an almost frenzied manner to go to the defense of Jabesh-gilead, 1 Samuel 11. Possibly Saul's zeal is explained by the fact that he might have had relatives in Jabesh-gilead—perhaps his mother or wife came from there. (The Benjaminites got their wives from Jabesh-gilead.) After Saul committed suicide at the Battle of Gilboa, the men of Jabesh-gilead showed compassion toward Saul in that they disposed of his body in an acceptable manner; see 1 Samuel 31. Furthermore, after Saul's death, David sent a subtle message to the men of Jabesh-gilead (supporters of Saul) suggesting that they link up with him, 2 Samuel 2:4–7. They did not accept David's invitation, but made Saul's son, Ish-bosheth, king of the northern part of the Promised Land, 2 Samuel 2:8–10.

Judges contains many significant details about the political, social, and religious conditions of the period it describes—details that make subsequent events in Israel's history more intelligible.

1 The problem of Israel's neighbors

That the Israelites managed to survive during their early years in Canaan is remarkable in view of the persistent hostility of their neighbors. Genesis has reason to describe the origins and character of Israel's neighbors as it does. (See **ILLUSTRATION 5D**.)

2 What kind of political structure did Israel have during this period?

Apparently Israel was organized the same as several other nations in the world of that time. A number of tribes (sometimes six and sometimes twelve) were loosely bound together on the basis of a common religious bond. The focal point was a central shrine, and the tribes were rostered to care for it. Religious festivals were held at this center, and the basic laws that directed the life of the tribes were formulated and administered there also.

The existence of this kind of organization during the period of the judges is suggested in Joshua 24. There are also indications that Israel did not always act as a unified whole, and that not all the tribes took part in the campaigns of the judges. The Song of Deborah berates the tribes of Reuben, Gilead (Gad), Dan, and Asher for their absence in the campaign against Jabin, 5:16–17. Gideon operated with men from only some of the tribes, 7:23. Samson operated as a one-man army.

3 Holy wars

The wars conducted by the judges were deemed Holy Wars, just as the invasion of Canaan under Joshua was viewed as holy. The duty to join in battle against Israel's foes was a solemn one. The Israelites were summoned to face powerful foes for which they were often no match, 5:8. But the Lord fought for Israel from the heights of heaven (5:20), and used heavenly weapons such as rainstorm and flood against Israel's foes.

Ultimately Israel's battles were not fought against the Canaanites, Ammonites, Moabites, Midianites, and Philistines, but against the gods and goddesses of these peoples. The real enemies of Israel were the Baals and Ashtaroth, Dagon, Chemosh, and the other gods of the region. But "the Lord conquered" is how the scriptures state it, and that said volumes to the people of Israel.

4 The adjustment from nomadic to agricultural Life

The Hebrew people had to make a profound adjustment as they switched from a nomadic lifestyle in the wilderness to a more settled agrarian style of life in Canaan. This adjustment involved more than just the mechanics of agricultural methodology. The Hebrews had entered a land in which the gods of nature were manipulated in religious rituals to ensure the fertility of land, livestock, and women. As they settled in Canaan, the Hebrews would have asked the local Canaanites about their farming methods. When they were told that fertility depended on the favor of the local gods, the temptation would have been strong to honor and worship those gods in the manner of the Canaanites. Judges says repeatedly that the Israelites did just that.

5 Reward and punishment

Judges stresses that the misfortunes that befell Israel were not just random events. They took place because "Israel did what was evil in the sight of the Lord" (4:1), and that evil was involvement in Baal worship. Here we see expressed the theological presupposition of the Deuteronomist: loyalty and obedience to God bring blessing and prosperity; disloyalty and disobedience to God bring trouble and judgment.

6. Lack of cohesion among the tribes

Not all tribes answered the call to join in battle against Israel's foes. The fact that the Moabites could cross the Jordan unhindered and wreak havoc in Benjaminite territory for 18 years suggests that no union of tribes existed to repel the oppressors, 3:12–30. Furthermore, the Ephraimites demonstrated a quarrelsome spirit on two occasions, 8:1–3, 12:1–6. Although Gideon used gentle words with them, Jephthah used sterner measures.

7. Kings—to be or not to be?

The judges were not kings. Their authority was neither absolute nor permanent. They established no personal dynasty, no administrative system, and possessed no standing army. It is possible that some within Israel felt that the judges could not deal with the threats facing Israel, and were suggesting that a king be appointed to help the situation. Gideon spurned the suggestion, 8:23. Although Abimelech assumed the role of king for three years, Jotham's parable (9:7–21) reflected the negative attitude of his subjects in relation to his kingship.

Chs. 17–21 reveal a different opinion on the subject of kings. They describe the moral and political chaos within the nation and make the repeated comment, "In those days there was no king in Israel; all the people did what was right in their own eyes," 17:6, 18:1, 19:1, 21:25. These comments suggest that some believed that the nation needed a centralized form of government to unify the tribes and address the issues of administrative and social anarchy.

THREE MAJOR PROBLEMS

The narratives in Joshua and Judges suggest that in the period following the conquest, the Israelites faced three major problems:

1. Political disunity

If the nation wished to retain its hold on the land, it would have to unite.

2. Dynastic continuity

The system of "here a judge, there a judge, everywhere a judge, judge" offered no continuity of rule. If the nation was to survive amidst hostile neighbors, it would have to establish a more stable system of government. A monarchy, perhaps?

3. Spiritual purity

Above all else, the Israelites needed to make up their minds about the challenge Joshua had set before them: "The Lord? Or Baal?" Joshua 24:14,15.

13A Passages in Joshua, Judges, and Deuteronomy describe the division of the land among the tribes who settled in the regions to the east and west of the Jordan River. Judges also describes counter-attacks and raids by the Moabites, Canaanites, Midianites, Ammonites, and Philistines.

13B Judges suggests that because the Israelites did not completely eliminate the Canaanites from the Promised Land, they intermarried with them and worshiped their gods.

13C The Israelites sought to deal with the problems they confronted within the land under the charismatic leadership of judges—military leaders and national saviors. Judges refers to twelve such leaders. Four of these were raised up when "the spirit of the Lord came upon them" (Othniel, Gideon, Jephthah, and Samson).

13D Each narrative reflects a similar framework:
- *Apostasy:* The people sin.
- *Battering:* God uses neighboring nations to discipline His people.
- *Cry:* Israel cries to the Lord for help.
- *Deliverance:* God raises up a judge to deliver the Israelites.

13E The writer focuses on the work of five judges in particular:
- Ehud
- Deborah (and Barak, her general)
- Gideon
- Jephthah
- Samson

13F Judges 17–21 contain two narratives that do not concern themselves with rule by judges, but with events and conditions of the period:
- The origin of the shrine at Dan, chs, 17,18;
- How 600 Benjaminites obtained wives after their tribe was all but wiped out, chs. 19–21.

13G Throughout the period of the Judges, the Israelites had to deal with a number of issues:
- The persistent hostility of neighboring nations;
- Internal needs;
- Dangers posed by the worship of false gods;
- Adapting from life as nomadic animal herders to life as settled grain growers;
- The impact their behavior had on whether they experienced "blessing or curse";
- The lack of cohesion among the tribes;
- Suggestions that there be a transition from rule by judges to rule by kings.

The people became increasingly aware that if they wished to secure a meaningful life within the Promised Land, they needed to establish:
- Political unity;
- Dynastic continuity;
- Spiritual purity.

CROSS WAYS

2 SECTION

UNITS 11–20

From the Conquest to the Babylonian Exile

UNIT 14

Kings—To Be or Not to Be?

From Judges to Kings

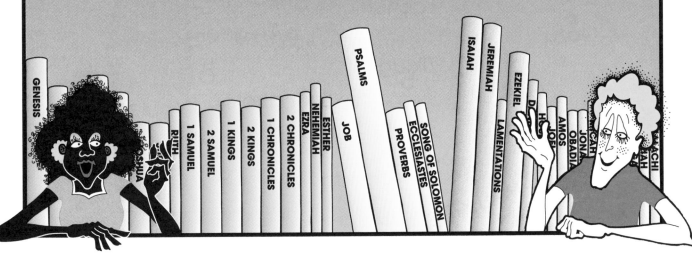

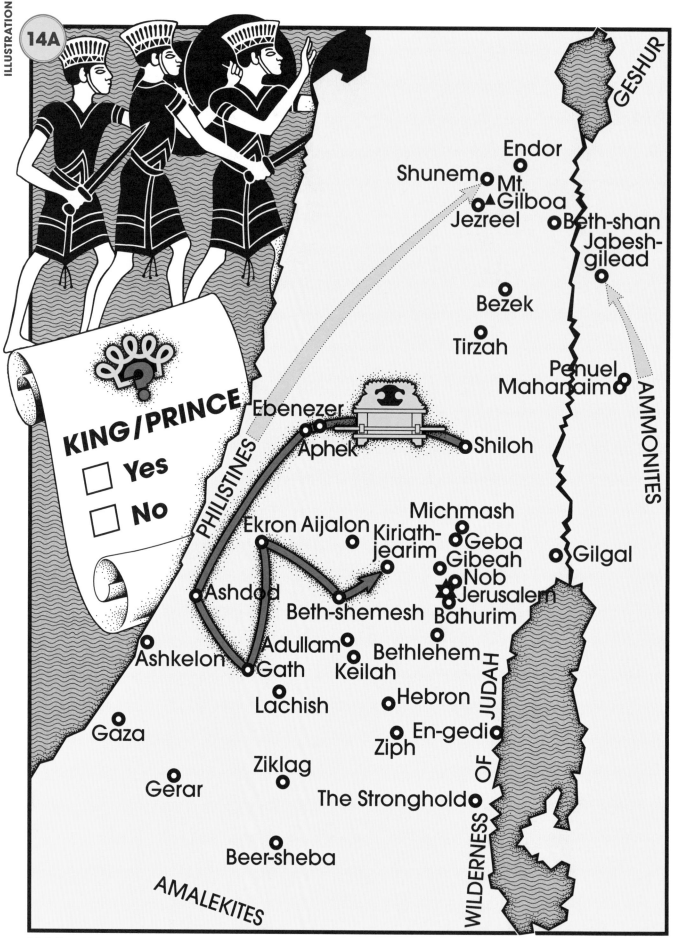

GESHUR

Endor

Shunem

Mt.
Gilboa

Jezreel

Beth-shan

Jabesh-
gilead

Bezek

Tirzah

Penuel
Mahanaim

AMMONITES

KING/PRINCE

☐ Yes

☐ No

Ebenezer

PHILISTINES

Aphek

Shiloh

Michmash

Ekron Aijalon

Kiriath-
jearim

Geba

Gibeah

Gilgal

Nob

Jerusalem

Ashdod

Beth-shemesh

Bahurim

Ashkelon

Adullam

Gath

Keilah

Bethlehem

JUDAH

Lachish

Hebron

Gaza

En-gedi

Ziklag

Ziph

Gerar

The Stronghold

WILDERNESS OF

Beer-sheba

AMALEKITES

First and Second Samuel were originally one book. They were divided into two books when the Old Testament was translated into Greek about 250 B.C. They outline Israel's history from the birth of Samuel to the time when David's life was drawing to an end—from about 1070–960 B.C.

The closing chapters of Judges refer to the increasing fragmentation of Israelite society. The lack of strong leadership had an adverse effect on the people: "All the people did what was right in their own eyes," Judges 21:25; see also Judges 17:6, 18:1, 19:1. The narrative in 1 and 2 Samuel points to David's kingdom as the legitimate successor to the tribal league, 2 Samuel 2:1–4; 5:1–5. The writer's belief is that God fulfilled His promises to the patriarchs through David.

The narrative in 1 and 2 Samuel is complex, particularly the sections that reveal different attitudes toward Saul and the institution of kingship. First Samuel 8 reflects a hostile attitude toward the monarchy; chs. 9 and 11 show a favorable attitude. First Samuel contains several accounts of how Saul became king, two accounts of Samuel rejecting Saul, two accounts of David being introduced to Saul, two accounts of David fleeing from Saul, and two accounts of David sparing Saul's life.

ILLUSTRATION 14A depicts some of the events and places referred to in 1 and 2 Samuel.

① Chs. 1–6: The opening scenes take place at **Shiloh**, where a shrine housing the **Ark of the Covenant** was located. After the **PHILISTINES** capture the Ark in a battle at **Aphek**, they take it to a number of Philistine cities—and in each case the inhabitants of those cities break out in boils (some translations suggest "hemorrhoids"). The beleaguered Philistines eventually send the Ark back to Israel. After a brief stopover in **Beth-shemesh** (6:12,19,20), it is welcomed and cared for in **Kiriath-jearim**, 6:21–7:2.

② Chs. 8–11: A debate arises concerning the need for a king of Israel; the terms **KING** and **PRINCE** are used in this debate. Saul is introduced in ch. 9 and viewed favorably.

③ In ch. 11, Saul, a farmer from **Gibeah**, rescues the people of **Jabesh-gilead** from the **AMMONITES**. There is reason to believe that either Saul's wife or his mother came from Jabesh-gilead, Judges 19–21; see Unit 13. On the way north to Jabesh-gilead, Saul summons the Israelite men to join him at **Bezek**, 11:8. After the Israelites under Saul rescue the people of Jabesh-gilead from the Ammonite threat, Samuel suggests that they take Saul to **Gilgal** and make him king, 11:12–15.

④ The number one enemy at the time was *Philistia*. The Philistines lived in five major centers: **Ashdod**, **Ashkelon**, **Gaza**, **Gath**, and **Ekron**. After being made king, Saul and his son Jonathan assemble soldiers from Gibeah and **Michmash** (13:2), and defeat the Philistines at **Geba** (13:3) and **Aijalon**, 14:31.

⑤ When David appears on the scene (13:14, ch. 16), Saul's days are numbered. Veiled conflicts arise between David and Saul. Although Saul had promised to give his *older* daughter, Merab, to any person who killed Goliath, Saul gives David his *younger* daughter, Michal, as his wife, 18:20–27. There are hints that Saul tries to kill David on his wedding night, 19:11–17.

⑥ David flees to **Nob** where the priest, Ahimelech, gives him holy bread from the sanctuary, along with Goliath's sword. Doeg the Edomite, one of Saul's servants, sees this happen and reports it to Saul, ch. 21. Saul orders Doeg to slaughter the priests at Nob for having helped David—which he does, killing 85 priests, plus men, women, children, infants, oxen, donkeys, and sheep. Only one priest, Abiathar, escapes with his life and then links up with David and his supporters, ch. 22.

7 Saul fails in his attempts to eliminate David, who eventually becomes a vassal of Achish (the Philistine king of Gath) and resides in *Ziklag*, 27:1–7.

8 Saul dies in a battle against the Philistines at *Mt. Gilboa*. Prior to the battle, the Philistine army camps at *Shunem*, 28:4. Saul uses a witch at *Endor* to conjure Samuel up from the abode of the dead so that he might consult with him concerning the outcome of the approaching confrontation, 1 Samuel 28. Samuel predicts Saul's death in the approaching battle.

9 After Saul sees that his sons have been killed and that the situation is hopeless, he commits suicide. The Philistines behead Saul and fasten his body to the walls of *Beth-shan*, 31:10.

10 The men of Jabesh-gilead rescue the corpses of Saul and his sons, take them back to Jabesh-gilead, burn them, and bury their remains, 31:11–13.

11 Some of the other places (depicted in **ILLUSTRATION 14A**) that play a role in the Saul/David and related narratives are:

> *Jezreel:* 1 Samuel 25:43; 29:1; 2 Samuel 2:8
>
> *Tirzah:* Joshua 12:24; 1 Kings 14:17; 15:21,33; 16:6,8,9,15
>
> *Ebenezer:* 1 Samuel 4:1–22
>
> *Geba:* 1 Samuel 14:5; some suggest Geba and Gibeah are the same place
>
> *Bahurim:* 2 Samuel 3:14–16; 16:5; 17:17–21
>
> *Adullam:* 1 Samuel 22:1
>
> *Bethlehem:* 1 Samuel 16:1,4 (David's birthplace)
>
> *Keilah*: 1 Samuel ch. 23
>
> *Hebron:* 2 Samuel 2:4; 5:1–11
>
> *Lachish:* Joshua 10:32; 2 Kings 18:13–17; 25:22–25
>
> *GESHUR:* 2 Samuel 2:3; 13:37; 14:23
>
> *Beer-sheba:* 1 Samuel 8:1–3
>
> *Ziph:* 1 Samuel 23:15,19
>
> *En-gedi:* 1 Samuel 23:29; 24:1
>
> *The Stronghold* (possibly Masada): 1 Samuel 22:4,5; 24:22

1 Samuel 1-6

Chs. 1–6 contain two stories that are closely related. Chs. 1–3 tell of the birth and call of Samuel, who will play a key role as priest, prophet, and judge in the narrative of chs. 7–29. Chs. 4–6 report how the Ark of the Covenant was moved from Shiloh to Kiriath-jearim. Eventually, David transferred it from Kiriath-jearim to Jerusalem, 2 Samuel 6. Finally, Solomon placed the Ark into the Temple he built to house it, 1 Kings 8.

1 1 Samuel 1–3 give details about Samuel's conception and birth, his consecration (by his mother, Hannah) for life in God's service, and his divine call and commission. Because Samuel played an important role in Israel's history, the writer considers it fitting that these details be known, 1 Samuel 1:1–20.

2 While Samuel is still quite young, his parents (Elkanah and Hannah) place him in the care of Eli, the priest at **Shiloh**, 1:21–28. Hannah thanks God for the gift of Samuel (2:1–10) and for the gift of "his king," 2:10. When, during the years that follow, Elkanah and Hannah make their annual visit to Shiloh, Hannah takes with her a linen priestly garment that she has made for Samuel, 2:18–20.

3 Eli's sons exploit the people (2:12–17), and are immoral, 2:22. It is possible that their immoral acts had to do with involvement in the sexual rites associated with Baal worship. Although their father disciplines them, they ignore him, 2:23–25. (The implication is that Samuel will soon replace Eli and his sons.) Eli is told that his house must soon come to an end, 2:31; see ch. 22. One of his descendants, Abiathar, will be spared but will lead a rather unhappy life. Solomon will send him into exile for supporting his brother Adonijah in his bid for the throne, 2:33; see 1 Kings 1:7; 2:26,27. At the same time, a "faithful priest" will eventually be spared to serve God's anointed, 2:35; that priest will be Zadok, 2 Samuel 8:17; 15:24; 1 Kings 1:8; 2:35.

4 The nature of the shrine at Shiloh is uncertain. It is called variously, "the house of the Lord," 1:7,24; 3:15; "the temple of the Lord," 1:9; 3:3; and "the tent of meeting," 2:22. Although it houses the Ark of the Covenant (3:3) and Samuel sleeps within the structure near the Ark, the shrine is never referred to as the Tabernacle.

5 The focus now becomes the Philistine threat, 4:1. The Israelites had been able to conquer Canaan because it was organized into city states and unable to offer unified resistance. They were able to maintain their hold in Canaan because the tribes rallied together to deal with the threats from within and beyond Canaan's borders. The **PHILISTINES** posed a different kind of threat. They were a well-organized, well-armed, and well-disciplined military people. When they set out to gain control of the lands on their borders that had gained freedom from Egyptian domination, the Israelites were faced with a serious problem.

6 1 Samuel 4 reports the Philistine advance into Israel. The decisive battle took place at **Aphek**, a Hebrew city near Philistine territory. Israel was forced to retreat. To bolster their morale, the Israelite forces sent for the Ark of the Covenant from Shiloh (4:3), but all in vain. The Israelites were defeated, and the Ark was captured. When news was brought to the aged priest Eli of the death of his sons in battle, of the military defeat, and of the capture of the Ark of the Covenant by the Philistines, he died, 4:10–18; note 4:18.

7 The Philistines took the Ark back to **Ashdod**—one of their principal towns. The narratives in chs. 5 and 6 indicate that the presence of the Ark caused the Philistines considerable trouble. Not only

did their god Dagon fall over on two successive nights and lose his head and arms (5:1–4), but the Philistines were afflicted with "tumors"—meaning either boils or hemorrhoids, 5:6.

 The result was that the Philistines made arrangements to return the Ark to Israel. Seven months of the presence of the Ark was enough! So, they built a new wagon to which they yoked two cows that had recently given birth to calves and had never pulled a cart. Their priests and diviners told them to load on to the wagon five golden replicas of the tumors as well as five golden images of the mice that were thought to have been associated with the plague, 6:1–9 (*five:* one for each Philistine city). Apparently the hope was that, as the Ark and the images left Philistia, so would the plagues. The Philistine cows headed straight for **Beth-shemesh** within the Promised Land. However, when many in the vicinity of Beth-shemesh lost their lives after the Ark's arrival, the Ark was sent to **Kiriath-jearim**—not to Shiloh, 7:1,2. Possibly, Shiloh had been destroyed, Jeremiah 7:12–14; 26:6–9.

1 Samuel 8-12

Prior to Saul being anointed as king (chs. 9–11), there are hints that possibly Eli and his sons, and Samuel and his sons, were hoping to gain a leadership position within the nation.

● **The House of Eli**

Eli was the leading priest at a shrine in Shiloh where the Ark of the Covenant was housed. His two sons, Hophni and Phinehas, served as his assistants. However, Hophni and Phinehas engaged in indecent sexual activities—possibly associated with fertility cult rituals. They were killed during a battle between the Israelites and Philistines, and the aged Eli died when he was told that the Philistines had captured the Ark of the Covenant. (See 1 Samuel 1:3,9; 2:12–17,22–25; 3:10–14; 4:1–18.)

● **The House of Samuel** (7:3–17)

First Samuel describes the life of Samuel in a positive manner, and suggests that he had considerable influence within the nation. In addition to his priestly duties, he played the role of a warrior-judge or military leader who won victory for God's people in time of crisis. Under his leadership, the Israelites gained a measure of independence from the Philistines.

Samuel's sons, Joel and Abijah, served as Judges at Beer-sheba, 8:1,2. However, they did not follow in Samuel's ways, but "turned aside after gain; they took bribes and perverted justice," 8:3.

When eventually the leaders of Israel met with Samuel and asked him to appoint a king over them, they stated that Samuel was old, and his sons were corrupt, 8:4,5. The people needed a ruler who would unify the tribes and lead them successfully into battle, 8:5,19,20. Samuel responded to the leaders' request by telling them that if they appointed a king, he would exploit and enslave them, 8:10–18. (Samuel's negative comments about kingship seem to reflect an awareness of how Solomon eventually exploited and enslaved his subjects.)

Despite the statement made in 7:13 that the Philistines were subdued and did not enter Israel's territory again during Samuel's lifetime, the continuing narrative states that the Philistines caused problems throughout Saul's reign and were only finally subdued by David. Perhaps the point of the chapter is that Israel does not need a *king* to fight its battles. God fights successfully for Israel through the one He chooses.

The debate about whether or not Israel should have kings now comes to a head. There are hints that the people suspected that the nation's problems could not be solved by "ecclesiastical power." The appointment of a king seemed essential if anything was to be done about getting rid of the Philistines who were already camped within Israel's borders (13:4) and were causing the people real problems, 13:19–23. Israel was faced with the choice of enslavement or seeking a way to cope with the Philistines. In the minds of many there was only one choice: "Let's have a king!" A succession of narratives describe how Saul finally made it to the throne.

 The *first series of stories* (1 Samuel 8; 12:1–25) reveals a negative attitude toward kingship. They suggest that the reason for the emergence of a king was that the people *demanded a king* because *they desired to be like the surrounding nations*. The spirit of these sections is reflected in 1 Samuel 8:7, "They have rejected me [God] from being king over them." The cry longs for the "good old days" of the theocratic state during the time of the tribal league. The way of kings was the way of Canaan. The office of king should not be bestowed on any man. In the surrounding nations the king was thought to possess divine power. In Egypt the pharaoh was venerated as a god, while in Mesopotamia the king was thought to be the representative of the gods, the adopted son of the gods. Nothing like this should ever happen in Israel! After all, God was their King!

 The *second series of stories* (9:1–10:27) says that when Saul's father, Kish, lost some donkeys, Saul went looking for them. Ironically, although Saul did not find the donkeys, he ended up with kingship! While searching for the donkeys, Saul sought advice from Samuel, a seer. God had previously told Samuel that He had chosen Saul to be the savior of the Israelites. Samuel accordingly anointed Saul as king in a secret ceremony. Immediately the new king joined ranks with a group of ecstatic prophets and experienced a kind of divine charisma while with them. In this narrative, Saul's office is defined as *prince*, 9:16, 10:1.

The secret selection and anointing of Saul as king is confirmed by the casting of lots, 10:17–27. Although there is nothing negative in the narrative concerning the casting of lots, the tone of 10:17–19 with regard to kings is quite negative. The suggestion seems to be that although the *Lord*, the Israelites' Heavenly King, had rescued them from the Egyptians and other enemies, and from a variety of calamities and distresses, the people were now placing their faith in an *earthly king*.

First Samuel 9:22–26 describes Samuel and Saul sharing a meal together. (It is significant that Saul eats with a *priest* at the beginning of his reign, but with a *witch* just prior to his death, 28:20–25.) The day after they ate together, Samuel anointed Saul into office as king, and the spirit of God came upon Saul, 9:25–10:13. The spirit of the Lord had likewise come upon four judges who had earlier delivered Israel, Judges 3:10, 6:34, 11:29, 14:6. Later, the spirit would come upon David, 1 Samuel 16:13. Although the Old Testament makes no reference to the spirit coming on any *king* after David, it speaks of the spirit of God coming upon *Jesus the Messiah*, Mark 1:9–11.

The *third narrative* (ch. 11) speaks of the Ammonites under Nahash setting siege to Jabesh-gilead in the Transjordan. The people of Jabesh-gilead could not cope with the threat, offered to surrender, and agreed to become slaves of the Ammonites. Nahash accepted the offer but demanded that their right eyes be gouged out as a symbol of servitude. The people of Jabesh-gilead asked for a respite of seven days to seek help from Israel, with the understanding that if no help was offered they would submit to the Ammonites. When Saul heard of this situation he was moved to passionate anger and, seized by the spirit of God (11:6), rallied the tribes of Israel to go to the help of their besieged kinfolk. Saul's campaign met with such resounding success that the people assembled at Gilgal and made Saul *king*. Saul had *demonstrated his ability to inspire, lead, and rule the Israelites!*

1 Samuel 13–15

Saul's elevation to kingship set the stage for the clash between *prophet-priest* and *king* that continued throughout the history of the monarchy. Samuel was apparently willing to support Saul as long as he confined his activities to that of a political and military leader. But when Saul gave indications of dabbling in the domain of prophet and priest, Samuel withdrew his support.

 The *first narrative* that deals with this issue is 1 Samuel 13:1–15a. Samuel tells Saul to go to Gilgal and wait seven days, after which Samuel will join him and offer sacrifice to the Lord as a preface to an Israelite campaign against the Philistines. When Samuel fails to show up on time at Gilgal, Saul offers the sacrifice. We might ask, "Why did Samuel arrive late?" But that misses the *theological* point that Saul—a *political leader*—dabbles in *priestly functions* and arouses the wrath of Samuel. In disobeying the *Lord's prophet, Samuel*, Saul shows himself disobedient to the *Lord*, and therefore his rule will not continue.

 1 Samuel 15 presents a *second account* of Saul's rejection. Despite his military victory over the Amalekites, Saul is depicted as a moral and religious reprobate, in that he did not completely destroy the accursed Amalekites and their possessions. Saul spared Agag, king of the Amalekites, and some livestock. Samuel displayed little inclination to grant Saul absolution when he confessed (15:24–26; but see also 15:31), and personally hacked Agag to pieces with a sword in the vicinity of a shrine at Gilgal to ensure that *all* the Amalekites were wiped out, 15:32,33.

The theological point is that Saul did not obey all the rules of Holy War. He should have wiped out all of Israel's enemies, Deuteronomy 25:17–19. However, he did not. He spared their king and some of their cattle.

Despite the events outlined in 1 Samuel 13,15, Saul continued to rule as king, and Samuel withdrew from the scene, 1 Samuel 15:34,35. Eventually Saul's position deteriorated to the point where he slew the priests of Nob (22:6–19) and consulted a witch at Endor, ch. 28. Indeed, the writer has made his point. No dynasty would issue from the family of Saul of Benjamin. The stage is set for David of Judah to make his appearance!

Several threads run through the narratives analyzed in 14C.

1 There is on occasion a shift in terminology from *prince* to *king*. It is possible that as the nation became increasingly aware of its inability to cope with the Philistine menace, it sought to increase the spirit of unity and cooperation among the tribes by appointing a single ruler, maybe a "super judge" or a "head of the tribes of Israel," 1 Samuel 15:17. However, as time passed and the nation became increasingly aware of how kings exploited their subjects (e.g., Solomon, 1 Samuel 8:10–18), bitterness developed toward the institution of kingship. The term *prince* invariably adopts a positive stance toward a national ruler; the term *king* denotes a negative stance. The term *prince* permits *God* to remain Israel's king. (Note: the RSV translates the Hebrew word *nagid* as "prince"; the NRSV translates *nagid* as "ruler." Both are possible, but the term prince points more meaningfully to the tension between the two words.)

2 Some of the narratives reflect not only a negative attitude toward the office of king, but also a power struggle between God's *prophets-priests* and Saul, the *king*. Samuel insists that a king should be subject to God's spokesman, but Saul acted contrary to this opinion, 1 Samuel 13.

3 There was another issue at stake in the debate. The judges had been charismatic persons, raised up and empowered by God's spirit to act in a specific situation. No judge established a dynasty. However, when kingship became the order of the day, the question of who would be the next leader was no longer an issue. The people got the king's oldest son as their next ruler, whether or not they wanted him, whether or not he was competent, and whether or not he cared about God or the people!

4 The writer wishes to stress that David's (not Saul's) kingdom is the legitimate successor of the tribal league. Debate about whether or not there should be kings in Israel ceases when Samuel anoints David, 1 Samuel 16:13. The question now becomes, "Whose dynasty?" The writer's answer to that question is: "David's!"

1 Samuel 13-2 Samuel 1

First Samuel 15 reports Saul's failure to destroy everything and everybody in the war against the Amalekites. The complex narratives that follow do not debate the rights and wrongs of having a king. They trace the *decline of Saul*, and the *rise of David*. They can be summarized as follows:

1 God tells Samuel to waste no time in secretly anointing David, the youngest of Jesse's seven sons, as king of Israel, 16:1–13. The spirit of the Lord then comes upon David, 16:13. The spirit of the Lord then departs from Saul, and an evil spirit from the Lord replaces it, 16:14.

2 David now enters Saul's service as his nerve-soothing musician and armor-bearer, 16:16–23. The chapters that follow contain a second account of how Saul first comes into contact with David— *after* David killed Goliath, 17:55–18:2. Surprisingly, according to 17:31–40, Saul and David had talked together *prior to* David's encounter with Goliath, and Saul had dressed David in his armor; see also 2 Samuel 21:19 and 1 Chronicles 20:5.

The David-Goliath narrative presents David as one who has unshakable trust in the Lord and who points to the Lord as the one who gives him the victory. David is portrayed as one who possesses the qualities necessary for kingship: courage, military skill, and faith and trust in the Lord. David knew how to fight a Holy War—God's way (as the Israelites understood "God's way").

3 The narrative in 18:1–4 is a significant one. Jonathan gives David tokens signifying that he will raise no objection to David succeeding his father, Saul, as king. Jonathan's actions are remarkable because, theoretically, he himself is next in line for the throne.

Perhaps the question of whether or not Jonathan would follow Saul is dealt with in Samuel 14. Although 1 Samuel 13:14 states that Saul's kingdom will not endure, it does not say whether Saul or a dynasty based on his line has been rejected. The point of the story might be that dynastic succession is out of the question for *Saul*. In their encounter with the Philistines, neither Saul nor Jonathan consults the Lord before confronting the enemy. Jonathan expresses the hope that the Lord is with him, but tells no one but his armor-bearer what he is planning to do. In the latter part of the story, Saul forbids the soldiers to eat before evening. Jonathan, not knowing of Saul's command, breaks it by eating honey; his actions were wrong, and he stands guilty. Perhaps *Jonathan* is not a suitable candidate for king.

4 David now becomes too successful and popular for Saul's liking. David proved such a splendid warrior that he was adored as a popular hero, and the people sang:

> Saul has killed his thousands,
> And David his ten thousands. (1 Samuel 18:7)

This chant compared Saul's ability with that of David. It aroused Saul's jealousy, and resulted in him seeing David as a potential rival for kingship, 18:8–16.

5 Saul had promised that whoever killed Goliath would be given his daughter in marriage. Although Saul should have given David his *older* daughter, Merab, he gave him his *second* daughter, Michal. However, before he handed Michal over to David, he demanded that David obtain one hundred Philistine foreskins for him, expecting that David would be killed in the attempt. David killed not one hundred but two hundred Philistine men to obtain double the number of required objects. When David produced the foreskins, Saul had to produce the bride, 18:20–29.

6 Jonathan refused to become involved in any of his father's schemes to kill David, 19:1. Instead, he did everything in his power to protect David from his father's wrath, 19:2–7. The narrative mentions several attempts by Saul to pin David to the wall with his spear, 18:10,11; 19:8–10.

7 Although it is at times difficult to establish the precise sequence of events in the Saul/David narrative, it appears that Saul tries to have David killed on his wedding night, 19:11–17. This time, Michal helps David escape. When Saul pursues David to Ramah (where Samuel is living) and Naioth, Saul and his soldiers lapse into a state of charismatic frenzy, 19:18–24.

8 David and Jonathan then engage in a tender conversation in which Jonathan promises David that he will inform him about Saul's intentions, ch. 20. Jonathan knows full well that his actions in support of David place him in danger; see 20:30–34. Although Jonathan knows that there will come a time when David has no more enemies—a time when David will himself be king—he makes David promise that he will not kill any of Jonathan's children, 20:12–17. Why did Jonathan feel the need to extract this promise from David? In the world of that time, when one dynasty took over from another, the practice was to kill the sons of the previous king to get rid of potential pretenders to the throne.

9 When on a later occasion David spares Saul's life while Saul is relieving himself in a cave in the region of En-gedi, Saul responds by acknowledging David's merciful action and by stating that he knows only too well that David will eventually be king. Saul also then extracts a promise from David not to kill Saul's descendants when he is made king, ch. 24; note vv. 20–22.

10 In fleeing from Saul, David goes to Nob where the priests help him by providing him with bread and a weapon in the form of Goliath's sword, ch. 21. David conceals from the priests information about his dangerous situation in relation to Saul, 21:2. When Saul finds out what the priests have done for David, he has them killed, 22:6–23. Only Abiathar escapes with his life, 22:20–23. The point appears to be that the priests favored David, not Saul.

11 After his visit with the priests at Nob, David flees to Achish, king of Gath, apparently hoping to find security under his patronage. (One might ask why David, who had recently killed Goliath of Gath, and with Goliath's sword strapped to his side, would have sought refuge with the king of Gath?) However, when Achish's servants suggest that David might be dangerous to have around, David realizes he is in danger, feigns madness, and escapes, 21:10–15. (Because madness was linked to demon possession, most likely Achish feared that, if he killed David, the demons would leave David's body and take up residence in his.)

12 David now flees to the cave of Adullam, southwest of Bethlehem (familiar territory for David), where a group of malcontents links up with him, 22:1,2. To ensure his parents' safety, David places them in the safe-keeping of the king of Moab at Mizpah, 22:3–5. (David's family tree went back to a Moabitess, Ruth 4:18–22.) Later, David slaughtered the Moabites, 2 Samuel 8:2.

13 David and his men go to the aid of Keilah and deliver its inhabitants from the Philistines. However, when Saul finds out about David's whereabouts and heads for Keilah, David flees the city lest its citizens hand him over to Saul, ch. 23. Abiathar joins David at Keilah, 23:6.

14 After fleeing from Keilah, David and his men move into the wilderness of Ziph, 23:14,15. Jonathan then visits David at Horesh and assures him that he will be the next king—adding that he, Jonathan, will be second to David, 23:15–18.

15 Although Saul pursues David in the wilderness of Ziph, his campaign must be abandoned when news of a Philistine incursion into his territory reaches him, 23:19–29.

16 For comments about ch. 24, see 8 and 9 above.

17 To support themselves, David and his followers operate a "protection business." When a man named Nabal refuses to pay David the required sum for services rendered, David plans to kill him—but

changes his mind when Nabal's wife, Abigail, pleads with David to have mercy on her foolish husband. When Abigail tells Nabal what she has done, Nabal conveniently dies soon afterwards, with the result that David sends for Abigail so that she (together with Ahinoam) might become his wife, ch. 25; note 25:43. The writer adds the important note that after David flees from Saul, Saul gives Michal, David's first wife, to Palti, son of Laish who is from Gallim, 25:44. Naturally, David will be troubled by the loss of Michal to Palti, for if she bears a child to her new husband, Saul might have another male descendant!

It is worth noting that a woman named Ahinoam was the mother of David's son, Amnon, 2 Samuel 3:2–5. Had this Ahinoam formerly been a wife of Saul, 1 Samuel 14:50? Possibly so. After all, claiming a king's harem was an act associated with claiming that king's throne.

18 Ch. 26 contains what appears to be another version of the narrative outlined in 1 Samuel 23:14–24:22. Although in this version of the story David is in a position to have Saul killed, he refrains from this. In the ensuing conversation-from-a-distance, David begs Saul not to compel him to live in territory beyond the borders of Judah, where he would be forced to serve other gods and run the risk of having to die away from the presence of the Lord, 26:17–20.

19 Ch. 27:1–7 has David making overtures once again to Achish, king of Gath—this time, successfully. Achish gives David the town of Ziklag for his personal use, 27:6. Although David tells the Philistines that he is attacking Judah to the east, the truth of the matter is that he is attacking the Amalekites to the south and making every effort to annihilate them, 27:8–12. David has not really joined forces with the Philistines; he is annihilating his own people's enemies, the Amalekites.

20 Ch. 28 sets the stage for Saul's death. First, reference is made to Samuel's death at Ramah, 28:3. Second, the Philistines march north to prepare to engage Israel in battle at Mt. Gilboa. Full of foreboding, Saul consults a witch at Endor, who brings Samuel back from the dead to reveal to Saul what is anything but good news. Samuel says that because Saul did not kill all the Amalekites (ch. 15, Saul spared Agag), Saul will lose the next day's battle against the Philistines, and Saul and his sons will lose their lives.

The Saul narrative is "book-ended" by narratives that have to do with eating together—an act which, in the culture of the day, would bond people together as if they were family. In 1 Samuel 9:22–10:1, we read of Saul eating with Samuel, a *prophet*. On the evening prior to his death, Saul eats in the home of a *witch*, 1 Samuel 28:21–25.

21 David's situation in relation to the coming battle between the Philistines and Israel is awkward. If he fights with the Philistines against his own people, his chances of becoming king will be over. However, while Achish is prepared to partner with David in the coming battle with the Israelites, the other four Philistine kings vote to send David back to Ziklag. Without doubt, David is delighted with this turn of events, ch. 29; *he does not have to fight against his own people*. Furthermore, he separates himself geographically from any involvement with events leading up to Saul's death.

22 When David returns to Ziklag, he finds that the Amalekites have plundered and burned it, and taken captive everyone in it—including all the women among whom were David's two wives, 30:1–5. David's people are so angry with him that they contemplate stoning him to death, 30:6. However, David manages to resolve the situation, to deal with the Amalekites, and to rescue those taken captive, 30:7–25.

23 Again, every action David takes in this battle with the Amalekites speaks well of him. He consults the Lord, and he shares the booty equally among the warriors, 30:21–25. And at a very opportune time, he sends gifts far and wide to his friends, the elders of Judah (who will soon need a new king!), 30:26–31. David's total success contrasts dramatically with Saul's total failure.

24 The Israelites lose the battle against the Philistines at Mt. Gilboa. Saul's sons, Jonathan, Abinadab, and Malchishua are killed. Saul commits suicide. The Philistines decapitate Saul and fasten his body to the walls of the city of Beth-shan as a final token of derision, 31:1–13.

25 Saul's career begins with him showing mercy to the men of Jabesh-gilead, 1 Samuel 11. It ends with the men of Jabesh-gilead showing mercy to Saul. They take possession of the bodies of Saul and his sons, burn them, and bury the remains respectfully.

Second Samuel 1 contains another account of Saul's death. It is likely, however, that the account in 1 Samuel 31 is the correct one, and that the young Amalekite was twisting the truth in the hope of currying favor with David. Perhaps the reason for this second account is to set the stage for David's lament for Saul and Jonathan. It also explains how David came into possession of Saul's crown and bracelet, even though he had nothing to do with Saul's death.

The way is now clear for David to make his bid for the throne!

1 First Samuel 8–29 offers a rather hazy picture of the first king of Israel. These chapters tell us virtually nothing about Saul's early years. When we first meet Saul, he is an adult man of impressive stature. Despite the negative tone that 1 Samuel often adopts towards Saul, he must nevertheless have had real leadership ability. He managed to pull the Israelite tribes together and accomplished considerable feats against those who had been harassing them, 1 Samuel 14:47,48.

2 It is significant that 1 Samuel makes no reference to Saul exploiting his subjects in any way—building himself a palace, making use of slave labor, levying taxation of any kind, collecting numerous wives, and gathering a harem. We hear of only one wife, Ahinoam, and one concubine, Rizpah; see 1 Samuel 14:50; 2 Samuel 3:7.

3 There are indications that even after Saul's death, a group remained fiercely loyal to his memory, 2 Samuel 16:5–14; ch. 20. There must have been reason for this. Certainly, later kings had more opulent tastes and showed a readiness to exploit their subjects to satisfy those tastes, 1 Samuel 8:10–18; 1 Kings 12:1–4,14,15.

4 Admittedly, there are also indications in 1 Samuel that Saul was one who responded quickly and with intense feeling to the situation at hand. His reaction to the plight of the men of Jabesh-gilead (1 Samuel 11), his slaughter of the priests of Nob (1 Samuel 22), and his hatred of David reflect this aspect of his personality. When Saul felt that the Lord had finally forsaken him, he emerged as a pathetic figure seeking some way of healing the rift and obtaining guidance for his campaigns, 1 Samuel 28. Even so, he was certainly willing to seek God's mercy and forgiveness, 1 Samuel 15:24,25.

5 First Samuel's account of Saul frequently points beyond Saul and the house of Benjamin to another dynasty and tribe—David and Judah, 13:14; 15:28; ch. 16. David's eventual accession to the throne is predicted by Jonathan (23:17), Abigail (25:28–31), Abner (2 Samuel 3:8–10), and even by Saul himself, 1 Samuel 20:30,31; 24:20. After David defeated Goliath, the impression prevails that a change in dynasty is only a matter of time.

14A 1 and 2 Samuel contain a detailed narrative about Eli and his sons, Samuel and his sons, Saul's appointment and reign as king, and the tensions between Saul and his successor, David.

14B In the opening chapters of 1 Samuel, the Ark of the Covenant is located in a shrine at Shiloh where it is cared for by a priest, Eli, and his two sons. Eventually the youthful Samuel joins the staff of the Shiloh sanctuary. After the Philistines conquer the Israelites in a battle at Aphek, they take the Ark to Philistia and place it in a shrine at Ashdod, and then in several other shrines. However, because the presence of the Ark causes them great discomfort, the Philistines send it back to Israel, where it is eventually housed in Kiriath-jearim.

14C After Eli's two sons are killed and Eli dies, and Samuel's sons are discredited, the cry goes up, "Give us a king!" Samuel first anoints Saul—a Benjaminite—as king in a private ceremony, and then anoints and eats with him publicly. Eventually Saul demonstrates his leadership abilities by delivering the people of Jabesh-gilead when the latter are threatened with extinction by the Ammonites. Saul establishes Gibeah in Benjamin as his capital city.

14D In the narratives in 1 Samuel 8–12, the term *prince* is viewed positively. After all, if the earthly ruler is viewed as a *prince*, then God is not dethroned as *King*. The term *king* is used both positively and negatively. In places, the narrative in 1 Samuel suggests that there is something of a power struggle between priestly and political authorities.

Saul falls from favor for two reasons. *First*, he performs a ritual that only a priest should perform, 1 Samuel 13. *Second*, he fails to annihilate all the Amalekites in a battle; he spares the life of their king, Agag, 1 Samuel 15.

14E After Saul falls from divine favor, David appears on the scene (1 Samuel 16) and is portrayed as one who will eventually supplant Saul. David proves himself to be a brilliant fighter, a capable leader, and one who knows how to deal with political challenges in a self-serving manner.

14F The narrative in 1 Samuel reveals nothing about Saul's early days. He is anointed as king soon after he appears on the scene. No reference is made to Saul building himself a palace, making use of slave labor, imposing a taxation system on his subjects, or having numerous wives and concubines. Even after his death, some remain fiercely loyal to his memory. Even so, throughout the narrative, there are numerous hints that it will only be a matter of time before David of Judah succeeds Saul of Benjamin.

When Saul finally loses his life during a battle with the Philistines at Gilboa, the men of Jabesh-gilead, whom Saul had rescued from the Ammonites early in his career, show great respect by burying the bodies of Saul and his sons in an appropriate manner. The way is now clear for David to make his bid for the throne. 1 Samuel emphasizes that the divine choice rested on David—not Saul. Only through David would God's promises to the patriarchs be fulfilled.

David eventually made it to the throne of Israel without having to resort to brutal measures to achieve that goal.

CROSS WAYS

2 SECTION

UNITS 11–20

From the Conquest to the Babylonian Exile

UNIT 15
David

The Kingdom of David: A Dream Fulfilled

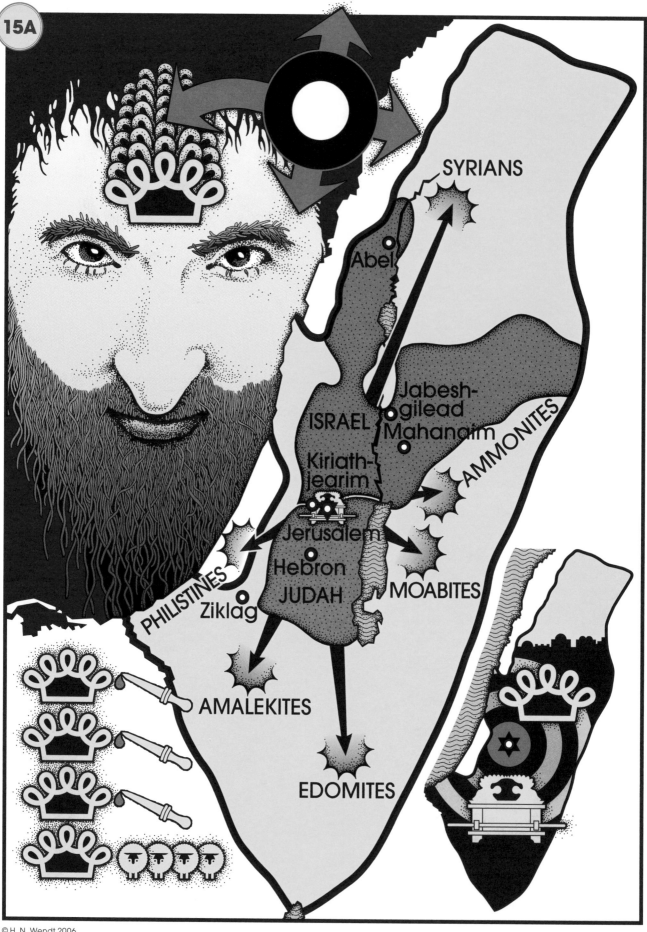

SYRIANS

Abel

Jabesh-gilead

ISRAEL

Mahanaim

Kiriath-jearim

AMMONITES

Jerusalem

Hebron

JUDAH

MOABITES

PHILISTINES

Ziklag

AMALEKITES

EDOMITES

Unit 15 studies the life of David outlined in 1 Samuel 13:14–1 Kings 2:9. Unit 31 will analyze the Chronicler's version of the life of David. **ILLUSTRATION 15A** summarizes David's reign. All passages quoted are from 2 Samuel, unless otherwise indicated.

1 After Saul's death, David was made king of **JUDAH** at **Hebron**, 2:1–4. No doubt the presence of his two wives, Ahinoam and Abigail, influenced the move to have David anointed as king. Ahinoam had apparently been Saul's wife, 1 Samuel 14:50; 25:43. Abigail, the widow of Nabal, inherited much territory in Judah after her husband died in a drunken stupor, 1 Samuel 25; note vv. 36–42.

2 Although David suggested to the people of **Jabesh-gilead** that they make him king of what had been Saul's entire realm, they refused, 2:4–7. Instead, Abner, Saul's general and cousin, made Saul's son, Ish-bosheth, king of what became known as the Northern Kingdom of **ISRAEL** at **Mahanaim**, 2:8–11. After Ish-bosheth's murder (ch. 4), David gained control also of the northern region, 5:1–5.

3 David moved his capital from **Hebron** to **Jerusalem**, located on the border between the two formerly separate realms, 5:6–10.

4 David brought the **Ark of the Covenant** from **Kiriath-jearim** to **Jerusalem** and placed it into a tent he had built to house it, ch. 6; note v. 17.

5 After building himself a palace, David felt moved to build God a new house—a temple. However, God assured David that He did not want or need a temple. Instead, God told David that He would make a house—that is, a *dynasty* or *line of kings* (**row of crowns**)—out of him, 7:1–17.

6 Next, David greatly expanded his kingdom by brutalizing neighboring nations (**SYRIANS**, **AMMONITES**, **MOABITES**, **EDOMITES**, and **AMALEKITES**) and incorporating them into his realm, chs. 8 and 10. Although David subdued the **PHILISTINES** once and for all (5:17–25), he did not make Philistia part of his kingdom. Prior to Saul's death, David had lived for sixteen months at **Ziklag** as a vassal and ally of Achish, the Philistine king of Gath, 1 Samuel 27:1–7.

7 After David's adultery with Bathsheba (chs. 11 and 12), chaos broke out in his family circle. The question throughout is: Which of David's sons will succeed him as king? His oldest son *Amnon* rapes his half-sister Tamar, and is murdered by Tamar's full-brother, *Absalom*, ch. 13 (**crown 1 and dagger**, *lower left*). After Absalom revolts and is killed by Joab (chs. 15–18, **crown 2 and dagger**), Adonijah (**crown 3 and dagger**) makes his bid for the throne, but is upstaged by Bathsheba, Nathan the prophet, and Solomon (1 Kings 1,2; **crown 4**).

After David's adultery with Bathsheba and murder of Uriah, Nathan the prophet rebuked David by telling him a story about a rich man who owned many sheep, but when he needed meat for a meal to entertain a special guest he stole the one lamb a poor man owned. David responded by insisting that the rich man give the poor man **four lambs** (*lower left*), 12:1–6; see Exodus 22:1. Ironically, during his reign *David himself* lost four "lambs": *Bathsheba's first child* 12:15–19; his daughter *Tamar*, whom Amnon raped and disgraced, 13:1–22; then his son *Amnon*, ch. 13; then his son *Absalom*, 18:1–18.

8 See the *lower right section* of **ILLUSTRATION 15A**: The puzzling statement in 1 Samuel 13:14 that David (**crown**) was a "man after God's heart" means that David worshipped one God *in Jerusalem* (**star, bull's eye**). No matter what brutalities David was involved in, the narrative nowhere refers to him as one who worshiped false gods. Furthermore, he brought the **Ark of the Covenant** to Jerusalem (**skyline**). Solomon eventually placed the Ark into the Temple he built to house it—thus setting the stage for what would eventually become *one God in one place*.

DAVID, KING OF JUDAH

2 Samuel 1-4

1 With Saul and Jonathan (the natural successor) dead (1 Samuel 31), the field was wide open for David to make his bid for the throne. He demonstrated outward respect for the previous dynasty by killing the Amalekite who claimed to have finished off Saul (1:1–16) and by lamenting the deaths of Saul and Jonathan, 1:17–27. After attending to the necessary mourning rites, David began his moves.

2 Prior to Saul's death, David had curried favor with leaders from the cities of Judah by sharing with them the spoils of his raids, 1 Samuel 30:26. After Saul's death, he was promptly appointed king over this southern region, with Hebron as his capital, 2:1–4. The Philistines did not intervene. Possibly they saw no potential threat in David's move. After all, he had previously been an ally, 1 Samuel 27:1–7.

3 David now set out to win control over the northern tribes. His commendation of the men of Jabesh-gilead for burying Saul contained the subtle suggestion that they consider submitting to his authority, 2:4b–7. They answered by accepting Saul's son, Ish-bosheth, as king over them—with his capital at Mahanaim, 2:8–11. This move was engineered by Abner, who had been Saul's general. Abner was also Saul's cousin, and was therefore a blood relative of Ish-bosheth, 1 Samuel 14:50,51.

4 The event recorded in 2:12–32 is puzzling. The groups who faced one another at Gibeon came respectively from Judah and Israel (although 2:15 states that the northerners came from Benjamin). It seems that twelve soldiers representing Judah and twelve representing the northerners lined up facing one another near a pool at Gibeon, and at a given signal began fighting. The idea was that the group which still had some survivors at the end of the confrontation achieved victory for the larger group they represented; see 1 Samuel 17:8,9. However, the outcome in this particular contest remained undecided; all the champions died—the consequence of which was that the larger armies from both Judah and the north now had to engage in battle. Because Abner (Saul's general and now Ish-bosheth's general) killed Asahel, one of Joab's brothers, an ongoing war erupted between the house of David and Saul's descendants. The outcome was: "David grew stronger and stronger, while the house of Saul became weaker and weaker," 3:1.

5 The reader is now introduced to the wives who graced David's residence in Hebron, and to the three sons who played a key role in the struggle for succession: Amnon, Absalom, and Adonijah, 3:2–5.

6 David's cause was helped when trouble developed in Ish-bosheth's household. Apparently Abner took Rizpah, Saul's former concubine, for his own personal use. Ish-bosheth justifiably interpreted the action to mean that Abner had his eye on the throne; see 16:21,22; 1 Kings 2:22. The ensuing hostility resulted in Abner threatening to hand over the Northern Kingdom to David, 3:6–11. He contacted David about the matter (3:12–16) and discussed it with the northern elders, 3:17–19. He handled Benjamin with special care, 3:19. Abner then travelled south to carry out his threat. David had prepared a feast for Abner, and they ate together—an act which signified brotherly bonding and commitment to work together. Arrangements to enable David to gain control over the northern realm seemed to go well (3:20,21), until Joab threw a wrench into the works.

7 When Joab was told that David had met with Abner, he chastised David and insisted that Abner was acting as a spy. Joab then had Abner recalled and (apparently unbeknown to David) killed him, supposedly to avenge his brother's death, 3:22–30. David found himself in a difficult position.

Although Joab had killed Abner, David needed Joab's friendship and help to capitalize on the move Israel (and specifically Abner) had made to submit to his rule. If David could gain control of Israel, he could unite the kingdom. He managed to survive the crisis by a show of public mourning for Abner which convinced the north that Abner's death had been a blow to him, an event in which he had not been involved, and a tragedy which he sincerely regretted, 3:31–39. It is possible that Joab killed Abner because he knew that David would eventually gain control of a united kingdom and there would be room for only *one general* in the new realm. And Joab wanted to be that one general!

8 News of Abner's death had an unsettling effect on the northern tribes. Ish-bosheth was murdered and decapitated. Those responsible took his head to David hoping to win his favor, but were instead executed and suspended from a tree with their hands and feet cut off, 4:2,3,5–12.

DAVID, KING OF JUDAH AND ISRAEL

2 Samuel 5

1 After Ish-bosheth's death, the northern tribes made final arrangements to have David made king over Israel as well as Judah, 5:1–5. The narrative contains chronological difficulties. While the text suggests that David ruled Judah for seven and a half years before gaining control over Israel, 2:10 says that Ish-bosheth ruled for only two years. Who then ruled Israel for the other five and a half years?

2 David's next steps reveal shrewdness and insight. He captured the Jebusite stronghold of Jerusalem and made it his capital, 5:6–10; (see Judges 1:8,21; 19:10–12). The city was strategically located between Judah and Israel; it previously had been part of neither territory. This politically neutral city was to play a significant role in the history of that people David had now welded into one nation.

When David's armies surrounded Jerusalem, the resident Jebusites at the top of the fortress's walls taunted David, suggesting that even if the defending army consisted merely of blind and lame people, they could prevent David from capturing the city. However, after David's forces captured the fortress, David gave orders to kill the blind and the lame within its walls. After all, David hated the blind and the lame, 5:8! From that day forth, the blind and the lame were forbidden to enter the Temple (that Solomon eventually built)—until Jesus changed things completely, Matthew 21:14.

3 At this point, the Philistines began to take notice of what was happening. To have as a neighbor a David ruling over Judah was one thing. To have as a neighbor a David ruling over both Judah and Israel was altogether another thing. The Philistines therefore set out to deal with the situation. However, in the valley of Rephaim west of Jerusalem, David dealt them a military blow which brought the Philistines' harassment of Israel to an end, 5:17–25.

4 After dealing with the Philistines, David turned his attention to other nations bordering on Israel. In a series of campaigns he conquered the Moabites, Ammonites, Edomites, Amalekites, and Syrians, and incorporated their territories into his realm, 8:1–14; ch. 10. Those conquered suffered considerable loss of life in these campaigns, 8:2,5,13. Furthermore, thousands of horses were hamstrung, 8:4.

5 The change was tremendous. Although the Israelites had previously been a disorganized league of tribes struggling to retain a foothold in Canaan, David's kingdom was now the major power in the region.

David's Early Reign

THE ARK COMES TO JERUSALEM

2 Samuel 6

1 David had captured Jerusalem with his own private army, 5:6. The fortress became David's personal property and was called "the city of David," 5:9. His wisdom and shrewdness moved him to take another step. He had the Ark of the Covenant brought from Kiriath-jearim to Jerusalem, 6:1–19.

2 Jerusalem had now been established as the *political center* of Israel. The presence of the Ark of the Covenant made Jerusalem also the *religious center* of the nation. The Ark had been the religious symbol during the time of Moses and the tribal league. Its presence in the new capital of the new nation was a unifying factor of considerable importance. (The narrative in 1 Samuel 4:1–7:2 reports how the Ark of the Covenant went from Shiloh to Kiriath-jearim, called Baale-Judah in 2 Samuel 6:2.)

DAVID'S DEALINGS WITH THE HOUSE OF SAUL

1 David had married Saul's daughter Michal some time after he had been given a place within Saul's court, 1 Samuel 18:20–28. It is possible that the marriage was never consummated, 1 Samuel 19:11–17. After David was forced to flee from Saul, Michal was given to another man, 1 Samuel 25:44. When Abner began negotiations to have Israel come under David's control, David insisted that Michal be returned to him, 2 Samuel 3:12–16. The reason why her own brother, Ish-bosheth, cooperated in arranging this is a mystery, 3:14,15.

When the Ark of the Covenant was being brought to Jerusalem from Kiriath-jearim, David danced at the head of the procession. Michal saw David do this and accused him of indecent exposure, 6:16,20. The result was that she was never again invited to share David's bed, and therefore died childless, 6:23. No descendant of Saul would come from Michal to claim kingship over Israel!

2 Two important incidents are recorded in 2 Samuel 9 and 21; it is likely that the events recorded in ch. 21 took place before those outlined in ch. 9. The Gibeonites (see Joshua ch. 9) approached David with the request that he hand over to them seven sons of the man (King Saul) who had once planned to wipe them out as a people. David handed over to the Gibeonites two of Saul's sons and five of his grandsons, all of whom were hanged or impaled.

David was Saul's son-in-law. In handing over the two sons that Rizpah, Saul's concubine, bore to Saul, he was handing over two of his brothers-in-law. Furthermore, in handing over the five sons of Merab (Saul's older daughter), he was handing over five of his nephews.

3 It is likely that Jonathan's son, Mephibosheth, was brought before David (2 Samuel 9) after the events described in ch. 21. Jonathan had sworn an eternal loyalty to David (1 Samuel 18:1–4), and made David promise that he would not wipe out Jonathan's descendants when he became king, 1 Samuel 20:12–17. David eventually took care of Mephibosheth, who was crippled in both feet (despite the comment in 2 Samuel 5:8 that David despised the blind and the lame). Most likely David desired to keep a watchful eye on Mephibosheth and make sure that he would pose no real threat to David or his dynasty.

2 Samuel 7

1 After building himself a palace, David decided to build a more appropriate house for the Ark of the Covenant—a temple. (He had previously constructed a tent for the Ark in Jerusalem, 6:17.) However, the prophet Nathan, acting as God's spokesman, told David that he was not to build the Lord a "house" (*temple*); the Lord planned to build a "house" (*dynasty*) out of David, 7:1–17.

2 Several suggestions are made as to why David did not build a temple: 1 Kings 5:3–5 says that he was too busy to do it; 1 Chronicles 22:6–10 says his period of rule had been too brutal. However, 2 Samuel 7:1 says that David decided the time had come to build the Lord a temple because he now did have peace from his enemies. Deuteronomy 12:8–12 says that the appropriate time to build God a temple is when peace prevails.

3 The key to understanding 2 Samuel 7 is its play on the word "house." In 7:1,2 "house" means "palace." In 7:5–7,13 it means "temple." In 7:11,16, 25–27,29 it means "dynasty," and in 7:18 it refers to "family status."

4 Saul had belonged to the tribe of Benjamin. His accession to the throne took place amidst debate as to whether or not Israel should have a king. After David is introduced (1 Samuel 16), this debate comes to an end, and the central question now is, "Whose dynasty? That of Saul of Benjamin, or that of David of Judah?" Saul's sin resulted in his dynasty coming to an end, 1 Samuel 13:13,14; 15:1–28. David is now assured that his dynasty will continue forever—sin or no sin, 7:12,14–17,29.

5 2 Samuel 7:1–17 contains two puzzling elements:

- The first emerges when 7:6,7 is compared with 7:13. In the earlier verses, God suggests that He has always been content to live in a tent (the Tent of Meeting?), and prefers to be a mobile God who can move around among the people. The latter verse suggests that it will be up to Solomon to build the Lord a house. However, David's thanksgiving prayer (7:18–29) makes no reference to this prediction concerning Solomon, and 1 Kings 5:3 and 1 Chronicles 22:7,8 give their own reasons why building the Temple was to be left to Solomon. Some suggest that the first part of 7:13 was inserted by a later editor.

- The second has to do with the notion that David's dynasty would last *forever*, 7:13,16,29. The covenant God made with Abraham was one of *Divine Commitment*; in it, God made promises to the patriarch. The covenant which God made with David was similar. The spirit of the covenant was that David and his descendants would rule the nation of Israel forever. The days of short-term rule over Israel by charismatic judges were at an end. A line of kings was now established.

6 However, the kingdom split after Solomon's death—after which David's descendants ruled only the Southern Kingdom of Judah. Even the southern dynasty seemingly came to an end when Jehoiachin died in exile in Babylon some time after 560 B.C., 2 Kings 25:27–30; Psalm 89. The New Testament sees the dynasty restored and established "forever" with the birth of Jesus. Matthew 1:1 states, "An account of the genealogy of Jesus the Messiah, *son of David*, son of Abraham."

David proved himself to be a capable *military leader*. However, there are indications that he was not a very capable *family leader* within the royal household. Possibly David's real personality is reflected in the character of his offspring and in the ruthless tactics he employed to get what he wanted.

Second Samuel 3:2–5 and 5:13–16 list the names of David's wives, concubines, and children. 2 Samuel 11,12 tell the story of David and Bathsheba in a straightforward manner. In the David/Bathsheba episode, David was guilty of three major sins: *first*, adultery; *second*, he had Uriah, Bathsheba's husband, killed; *third*, although sexual relations were forbidden while the armies of Israel were on the battlefield, David had sexual relations with Bathsheba, 1 Samuel 21:4; Leviticus 15:18. Nathan made it clear that even the king was not exempt from the scrutiny of God, 12:1–25.

Although the question of David's continuing dynasty is raised in 2 Samuel 7, the narrative describing the eventual appointment of a successor begins in 2 Samuel 13 and concludes only in 1 Kings 2:46 ("So the kingdom was established in the hand of Solomon."). The narrative describes how, one by one, David's sons (listed below) lost their lives and claims to the throne—until finally Solomon emerged the victor.

Son one: AMNON

Amnon raped his half-sister Tamar, and two years later was killed by his brother Absalom, 13:1–33. (Absalom was a full-brother of Tamar.) To escape his father's displeasure, Absalom fled to his maternal grandfather, Talmai the son of King Ammihud of Geshur, 13:37; see 3:3 and 15:8. His exile lasted three years, 13:38. At stake in the Amnon/Absalom episode was not just Tamar's honor; Absalom was next in line for the throne.

Son two: ABSALOM

1 After Absalom had spent three years in exile, Joab arranged a ruse to bring about his return, 14:1–24. Although the king refused to meet with his good-looking son (14:25–27) for two years, he finally relented and an apparent, superficial reconciliation took place, 14:28–33.

2 Before long, Absalom set about wresting the throne from his father (15:1–12) even though the throne would have been his eventually. Although David had established a new dynasty, he had not laid down any laws of succession, 1 Kings 1:27. Possibly Absalom felt that just as he had already fallen out of favor with his father, something similar might happen again—or maybe he just could not wait to get the throne. Whatever the reason, he set about attacking a weakness in his father's administration: David's failure to set up a system for hearing complaints and settling legal disputes, 15:3,4.

It is also possible that the people of Hebron were not all that supportive of David. After all, David was guarded by paid mercenaries—who were Philistines. That called for the payment of wages, which in turn meant the levying of taxes. Because Absalom had been born in Hebron, the people of that city would have felt a bond with him—and perhaps hoped that he might use them as his bodyguard.

3 Within four years Absalom had enough supporters to have himself crowned king at Hebron—David's first capital and Absalom's birthplace, 15:10. David was forced to flee from Jerusalem, leaving ten concubines to care for the palace (15:16), and Zadok and Abiathar to care for the Ark of the Covenant, 15:24–29. The sons of Zadok and Abiathar would eventually convey information to David about developments in Jerusalem, 15:27,28; 17:15–20. As he fled, David was protected by his bodyguard of Philistine mercenaries, 15:18. Apparently David felt it would not be wise to entrust his personal security into the hands of his own people.

4 It is not clear why David's first action upon hearing about Absalom's rebellion was to flee from Jerusalem. However, the account of David's flight serves as a literary device to unify the entire section. David travels away from the city and meets a number of people along the way: Ittai the Gittite, 15:19–23; Abiathar, 15:24–29; Hushai, 15:32–37; Ziba, who talks to David about the alleged treachery of Mephibosheth, 16:1–4; Shimei (a Benjaminite who cursed David), 16:5–14; and Barzillai the Gileadite, 17:27–29.

After the rebellion is crushed, David returns to Jerusalem—meeting some of the same people: Shimei, 19:16–23; Mephibosheth, 19:24–30; Barzillai the Gileadite, 19:31–40.

5 One who joined forces with Absalom was Ahithophel, 15:12,30,31. Ahithophel was not only the wisest man in the realm, 16:23; he was also Bathsheba's maternal grandfather, 11:3; 23:34. When word reached David that Ahithophel had joined Absalom, David immediately sent Hushai to serve as his spy in Absalom's inner circle in Jerusalem, 15:32–37.

6 Just what happened in Jerusalem after David's departure is a little difficult to piece together. 2 Samuel 16:1–14 suggests that Mephibosheth saw David's absence as an opportunity to make his bid for the throne, although Mephibosheth's eventual defense seems convincing enough, 19:24–30. It is possible that Ziba, Mephibosheth's servant, was lying and hoping for personal gain, 16:1–4. Shimei's rebukes and curses (16:5–14) reflect loyalty to the memory of Saul.

7 There was no doubt about Absalom's own personal ambitions. He went to Jerusalem and took over his father's harem (16:20–22), thereby declaring himself to be Israel's king in place of David. The verbal tussle between Ahithophel and Hushai makes fascinating reading, 17:1–23. Had Absalom followed Ahithophel's advice, most likely he would have won the day. However, he chose to follow Hushai's advice, which in turn gave the advantage to David. Ahithophel was apparently now sure what the outcome of the revolt would be: Absalom's cause was lost! So Ahithophel went home, set his house in order, and hanged himself rather than fall into David's hands, 17:23.

8 Absalom's forces were defeated. Absalom was killed by the wily Joab who disregarded the king's orders to spare his son's life, 18:1–18. David's mourning for Absalom was so intense that Joab felt it necessary to tell the king that his grief was overdone. It was making a bad impression on those who had fought for David. After all, a military victory called for rejoicing, 19:1–8.

9 Although the Israelites of the northern region made overtures to renew allegiance to David (19:8b–10), David had to appeal to the people of Judah to submit to his rule once again, 19:11–15. He strengthened his appeal by replacing Joab with Amasa (who had been Absalom's general, 17:25) as commander of the army, v. 13; Amasa was also David's nephew, and therefore cousin to Absalom and Joab.

10 When returning to Jerusalem, David again encountered Shimei the Benjaminite—and declared him forgiven for having cursed the king, 19:16–23; see 16:5–14. However, David was possibly well-advised to do just that; Shimei was accompanied by 1,000 Benjaminites—who were most likely armed. However, on his deathbed David asked Solomon to kill Shimei, 1 Kings 2:8–10. David also accepted Mephibosheth's explanation of his actions, 19:24–30 (although with some misgivings, in that he divided Mephibosheth's land between Mephibosheth and his servant Ziba). One senses a spirit of distrust between the "northerners" and the "southerners," 19:41–43. Their sense of being two separate peoples was still very much alive. This final section sets the stage for the next rebellion, ch. 20.

 Second Samuel 20 describes yet another revolt. Another Benjaminite, Sheba the son of Bichri, summoned the north to break away from David's rule. His cry was: "We have no portion in David, no share in the son of Jesse; everyone to your tents, O Israel!," 20:1. David ordered his new commander, Amasa, to deal with the problem, but Amasa acted so slowly that David called on Abishai, Joab's brother, to do something about the situation. David would have expected Abishai to enlist the help of Joab, and he did. Joab first murdered Amasa (his cousin), and then pursued Sheba to the northern city of Abel. A woman in Abel of Beth-maacah advised her fellow citizens to cut off Sheba's head and throw it to Joab, which they did. Apparently the people concluded that Sheba should die rather than the whole town.

It is interesting to note that, according to 20:23–26, Joab is now back in charge of David's army, Benaiah is in charge of David's Philistine mercenaries, and Adoram is in charge of forced labor.

Son three: ADONIJAH

 Amnon is dead. Absalom is dead. Adonijah is next in line, 1 Kings 2:15. To complicate matters, David's continuing claim to the throne is now in doubt. The narrative in 1 Kings 1:1–4 describes a beautiful young woman, Abishag the Shunammite, being put into David's bed to keep him warm. This event is interpreted in several ways. Some believe that because the succession was still in doubt and no successor had been named, the possibility existed that Abishag might become pregnant and produce a son to follow David. (A debatable explanation; David was already very old.) Others point out that in the ancient world, a nation's prosperity and the fertility of its land were bound up with the sexual virility of its king. Just as it was important for a ruler to be a man of strength and beauty, it was also important that he be a man of sexual potency. When a ruler became impotent, he lost his authority to rule. A consideration of 1 Kings 1:4,5 suggests that David was found to be sexually impotent.

 Whatever the case may have been, Adonijah, David's oldest surviving son, made his bid for the throne. He was supported in this move by Joab and the priest Abiathar, 1:7. A celebration meal was arranged at En-rogel near Jerusalem, and an invitation to attend was sent to those on whom Adonijah felt he could rely. Solomon was not invited, nor was Nathan (the Jerusalem prophet), nor were those in command of David's bodyguards, 1 Kings 1:5–10.

Son four: SOLOMON

 When news of Adonijah's plan became known, Nathan the prophet reported what was happening to Bathsheba, and an intrigue resulted, 1 Kings 1:11–14. Bathsheba told the king that he had once promised (indeed, under oath!) that Solomon would be his successor, 1:15–21. (No mention is made of this promise in the narrative prior to this point.) Nathan put further pressure on David (1:22–27), until finally David declared Solomon to be his successor, 1:28–37.

 At David's command, Solomon rode on the royal mule to Gihon where Zadok the priest anointed him king, 1:38–40. Solomon then returned to Jerusalem in triumph. When Adonijah heard what had happened, he knew his cause was lost and sought sanctuary in the shrine at En-rogel. Solomon promised to spare Adonijah's life on condition that he pledge him his loyalty, 1:41–53.

David's Last Days

1 David's last days are described in 1 Kings 2:1–12. In his last recorded words, David told Solomon to see to it that both Joab and Shimei were put to death, and this was done, 2:28–46.

- Joab, David's general, was David's nephew and therefore Solomon's cousin;
- Shimei had cursed David when he fled from Absalom, 2 Samuel 16:5–14. When David was returning to Jerusalem after Absalom's revolt had been put down, David promised Shimei that he would not harm him, 2 Samuel 19:16–23.

Was it perhaps *Solomon* who wanted both men removed from the scene? After all, Joab had supported Adonijah in his bid for the throne, and Shimei was a Benjaminite, 2 Samuel 16:5–14.

2 Solomon's brother, Adonijah, who had been unwise enough to ask for Abishag the Shunammite (David's *concubine*) as his wife (1 Kings 2:13–18), was also killed; see also 2 Samuel 16:20–22. Solomon interpreted Adonijah's request as a hint that he would also lay claim to David's *throne*, and used this as a pretext to justify reneging on his earlier promise to spare Adonijah's life.

3 Abiathar the priest was sent into exile, 1 Kings 2:26–27; see also 1 Samuel 2:33 (Abiathar) and 1 Samuel 2:35,36 (Zadok).

4 1 Kings 1:48 says that Solomon took his place on the throne as co-regent even while his father was still alive; see also 2 Kings 15:1–5 where Jotham rules as co-regent prior to his father's death. By the time of David's death, Solomon was securely established as king.

15A The narrative outlining David's reign is detailed and complex. It describes David building a kingdom and establishing a capital city which continue to play an influential role in the world view of Abraham's present-day descendants, and in the minds of many Christians.

15B After Saul lost his life in the battle of Gilboa, the elders of Judah anointed David as their king—with his first capital at Hebron in the center of Judah. David's efforts to have those living in what had been the northern part of Saul's realm accept him as king proved fruitless. The northerners chose to appoint Saul's son, Ish-bosheth, as their king rather than David.

When Joab killed Abner, Ish-bosheth's general, and Ish-bosheth was beheaded by his own people, the northerners invited David to rule over Israel as well as Judah. Naturally, David said "Yes!" and moved his capital from Hebron to Jerusalem—which he captured from the Jebusites. (Hebron was in the center of Judah; Jerusalem was on the border between Judah and Israel.) David then subdued the Philistines, and expanded his borders by conquering the Moabites, Ammonites, Edomites, Amalekites, and Syrians.

15C Eventually, David transferred the Ark of the Covenant from Kiriath-jearim to Jerusalem—thus making Jerusalem the nation's *religious* as well as its *political* center.

Although Saul gave David his daughter, Michal, after David slew Goliath, there is reason to believe that the marriage was never consummated. No offspring from Saul!

David continued to show kindness to Jonathan's son, Mephibosheth—possibly to ensure that he made no bid for the throne.

Eventually there came the brutal day when David handed over two of Saul's sons and five of his grandsons to the Gibeonites—who impaled them, 2 Samuel 21. (Two of these men were David's brothers-in-law and five of them were his nephews.)

15D When David decided that the day had come when he should build God a Temple in Jerusalem, God responded by telling David that He did not want a Temple—a *religious house*. However, God would build a *political house*—a dynasty, a line of kings—out of David.

15E A brutal struggle took place among David's sons to succeed their father.

- Amnon, David's oldest son, raped his half-sister Tamar, and was then killed by his brother Absalom.
- Absalom (son two) eventually cried "Revolt!" in the hope of attaining the throne of Israel— but was eventually killed by David's general and his own cousin, Joab.
- When David finally became old (and possibly was found to be sexually impotent), Adonijah (son three) made his bid for the throne. Adonijah was supported in this move by Joab and the priest Abiathar, but was upstaged by Bathsheba and the prophet Nathan— who contrived to convince David that he had promised the throne to Solomon.
- Just prior to his death, David gave instructions for Solomon to be anointed as his successor.

15F In his last recorded words (1 Kings 2:1–9), David exhorted Solomon to walk in the ways of the Lord and to do that which was right—and then finally asked Solomon to kill Joab and also Shimei (a Benjaminite who had cursed him when he fled from Absalom, and whom David had assured that he would never harm).

Soon after Solomon came to power, he had Adonijah, Joab, and Shimei killed, and Abiathar the priest (who had supported Adonijah) sent into exile.

CROSSWAYS

UNITS 11–20

From the Conquest to the Babylonian Exile

UNIT 16
From One to Two

The Reign of Solomon and the Division of the Kingdom

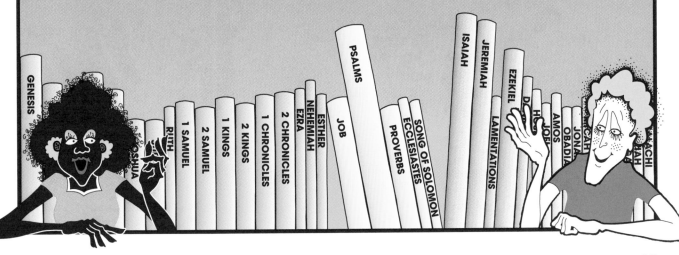

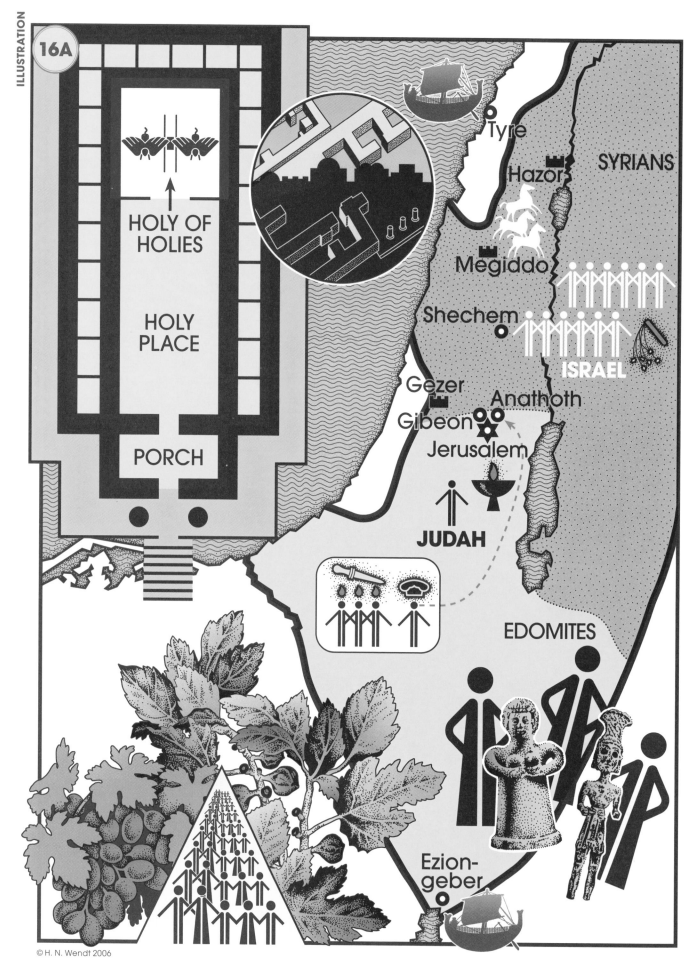

16A

HOLY OF HOLIES

HOLY PLACE

PORCH

Tyre

SYRIANS

Hazor

Megiddo

Shechem

ISRAEL

Gezer

Anathoth

Gibeon

Jerusalem

JUDAH

EDOMITES

Ezion-geber

© H. N. Wendt 2006

The Bible says less about the life of Solomon than it does about the life of David. Although other royal biographical materials once existed, they have not survived (e.g., *The Book of the Acts of Solomon*, 1 Kings 11:41; *The Book of the Chronicles of the Kings of Judah*, 1 Kings 14:29; *The Book of the Chronicles of the Kings of Israel*, 1 Kings 14:19). Information available today comes primarily from 1 and 2 Kings and from the later books of 1 and 2 Chronicles.

THE EARLY YEARS (ILLUSTRATION 16A)

1 Kings 1–11

1 Solomon succeeded his father, David, as king of a *united **ISRAEL** and **JUDAH***. As with David, Solomon's capital city was ***Jerusalem***, 1 Kings 2:10,11.

2 ***Dagger and drops of blood above three figures:*** Immediately after succeeding his father as king, Solomon gave orders for three men to be killed:
- His older brother *Adonijah* (2:13–25), who had sought to succeed David as king, 1:5–10;
- *Joab* (David's nephew and general, and Solomon's cousin), who had supported Adonijah in his bid for the throne, 1:7; 2:28–35;
- *Shimei* the Benjaminite who had cursed David when he was fleeing from Absalom, 2 Samuel 16:5–14; 2 Samuel 2:36–46. Although David later gave Shimei his word that he would not harm him (2 Samuel 19:16–23), on his deathbed, David commanded Solomon to kill Shimei, 1 Kings 2:8,9.

Fourth figure wearing priest's hat; arrow pointing to Anathoth: Solomon also sent *Abiathar*, a priest, into exile in **Anathoth**. Abiathar had supported Adonijah in his bid for the throne (1:7; 2:26,27).

3 ***Female figures; male and female idols:*** To ensure political alliances and peaceful relations with surrounding nations, Solomon married many *foreign women*. The first such marriage to receive mention was that to the daughter of the Egyptian Pharoah, 3:1. According to 1 Kings 11:1–8, Solomon also married Moabite, Ammonite, Edomite, Sidonian, and Hittite women—who brought with them their *false gods*.

4 ***Gibeon, Jerusalem, lamp (symbol of wisdom):*** 1 Kings 3:2 states that, at the beginning of Solomon's reign, the people worshiped at the "high places" because no house had yet been built for the name of the Lord. It is important to note that, after the Jerusalem Temple was built, the day eventually came when any other worship site was viewed as a high place—that is, as an *invalid worship center*. According to 3:6–9, Solomon went to **Gibeon** to the north of Jerusalem to offer sacrifice, and to pray for wisdom to distinguish right from wrong in order to rule his people effectively. After God granted Solomon's request for wisdom, he immediately offered sacrifice in ***Jerusalem***, 3:15.

Although Solomon is commended for not asking for the lives of his enemies (3:11), there was no reason for him to request this; he had already had them killed, 2:13–46.

Later, Solomon's wisdom is equated with his great knowledge (4:29–34) and his ability to answer all questions, 10:1–10.

5 Solomon undertook many building projects. The Phoenician king, Hiram of ***Tyre***, provided materials and artisans to help with these projects, 5:1,7–12. Solomon built numerous structures in Jerusalem itself (***buildings within circle***, *top center*), 7:1–8. The most famous of these was the **Temple** (*top left*), ch, 6. Solomon placed ***two cherubim*** (most likely, *winged oxen*) and the **Ark of the Covenant** into its *inner sanctuary*, the **HOLY OF HOLIES**, 6:23–28; 8:4–8. (See also **ILLUSTRATION 16C**.)

6 Solomon built ***fortresses*** at ***Hazor***, ***Gezer***, and ***Megiddo***, 9:15–19. He stationed 1,400 chariots and 12,000 ***horses*** (*near Megiddo*) in his chariot cities—including Jerusalem.

7 ***Ship near Ezion-geber:*** Solomon built a fleet of ships at ***Ezion-geber*** in partnership with the Phoenicians, and undertook trading ventures from there, 9:26–28; 10:11,12. The Phoenicians were a sea-faring people (***ship near Tyre***); the Israelites were not. Solomon's partnership with the Phoenicians also gave him access to markets around the Mediterranean Sea, 10:22.

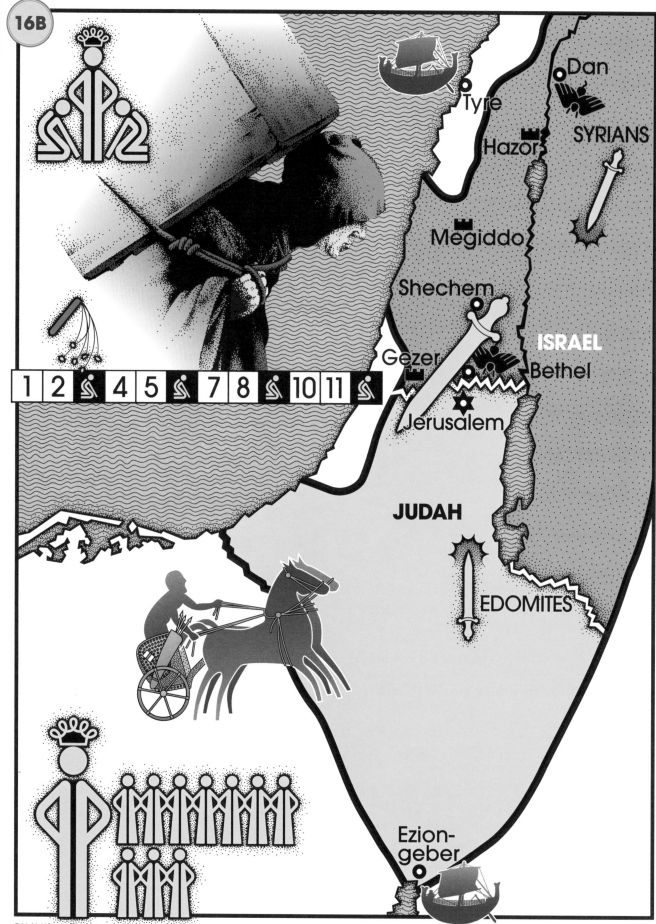

1 2 🛐 4 5 🛐 7 8 🛐 10 11 🛐

Tyre

Dan

SYRIANS

Hazor

Megiddo

Shechem

Gezer

ISRAEL

Bethel

Jerusalem

JUDAH

EDOMITES

Ezion-geber

8. *Twelve figures, whip, above ISRAEL; one figure above JUDAH:* Solomon did away with all traces of the former Tribal League. He placed 12 officials over the northern region of Israel, and one official over Judah. Eventually, the men in Israel were subjected to forced labor (*whip*), 1 Kings 4:6-19.

9. *Expanding triangle containing parents and children (lower left):* According to 1 Kings 4:20, the number of people within Solomon's territory was great in number—as numerous as the sand by the sea.

10. *Grapes on vine; figs on fig tree (lower left):* Throughout the length and breadth of Solomon's realm, his subjects ate and drank and were happy; they could rest beneath their *vines* and *fig trees*—and enjoy the abundance of fruit they produced, 4:25.

THE LATTER YEARS (ILLUSTRATION 16B)

1. *Crowned male figure; seven female figures, three female figures (lower left):* According to 1 Kings 11:1–8, Solomon (*crowned male figure*) had 700 wives (*seven female figures*) and 300 concubines (*three female figures*). These women came from Egypt, Moab, Edom, Ammon, Sidon (in Syria), and Hittite territory—and brought their gods with them:
   - *Astarte* from Sidon;
   - *Milcom* from Ammon;
   - *Chemosh* from Moab;
   - *Molech* from Ammon (the worship of whom involved the practice of child sacrifice).
   Solomon's foreign wives eventually persuaded him to worship their gods, 1 Kings 11:4. Solomon not only worshiped these false gods; he built shrines where they could be worshiped, 11:7,8. Solomon certainly did not walk in the ways of David, his father, 11:6; he did not worship *one God in one place*!

2. *Chariot and horses:* 1 Kings 10:26–29 describes Solomon buying horses and chariots from the Egyptians, and then selling them to the Syrians and Hittites. He was an arms merchant.

3. *Person carrying building materials; whip; slave on every third frame of 12-month calendar (top left):* Solomon used *forced labor* to carry out his building ventures, requiring the men of his realm to devote *every third month* to working on his projects—without pay, 5:13,14.

4. *Crowned Solomon; slaves to his left and right (top left corner):* It would seem that Solomon focused on having his people serve him rather than on devoting life to serving his people.

5. Because of Solomon's disobedience and polytheism, God incited the **EDOMITES** (11:14–22) and the **SYRIANS** (11:23–25) to revolt (*swords*) against Solomon and regain their independence.

6. *Large sword, jagged lines dividing realm:* The prophet Ahijah the Shilonite told Jeroboam, Solomon's chief taskmaster in the north, that after Solomon's death, the northern section of the realm would break away and become an independent nation—with Jeroboam as its first king. After hearing about Ahijah's prediction, Solomon sought to kill Jeroboam—who fled to Egypt, 11:26–40.

7. After Solomon's death, when Solomon's son, Rehoboam, told the northerners that he would rule them even more harshly than Solomon had done, the nation *split into two parts*. The Northern Kingdom made Jeroboam its first king; he reigned first at **Shechem**. Because Jeroboam could not permit his people to continue to worship in the Jerusalem Temple (it was located in the capital city of a foreign realm!), he built shrines at **Dan** and **Bethel** and commanded his subjects to worship at those shrines, 12:25–33. Although the *calves* Jeroboam placed in these shrines are referred to as idols, possibly they were **cherubim** similar to those in Solomon's Temple. Dan and Bethel were most likely *rival* shrines, rather than *pagan* shrines.

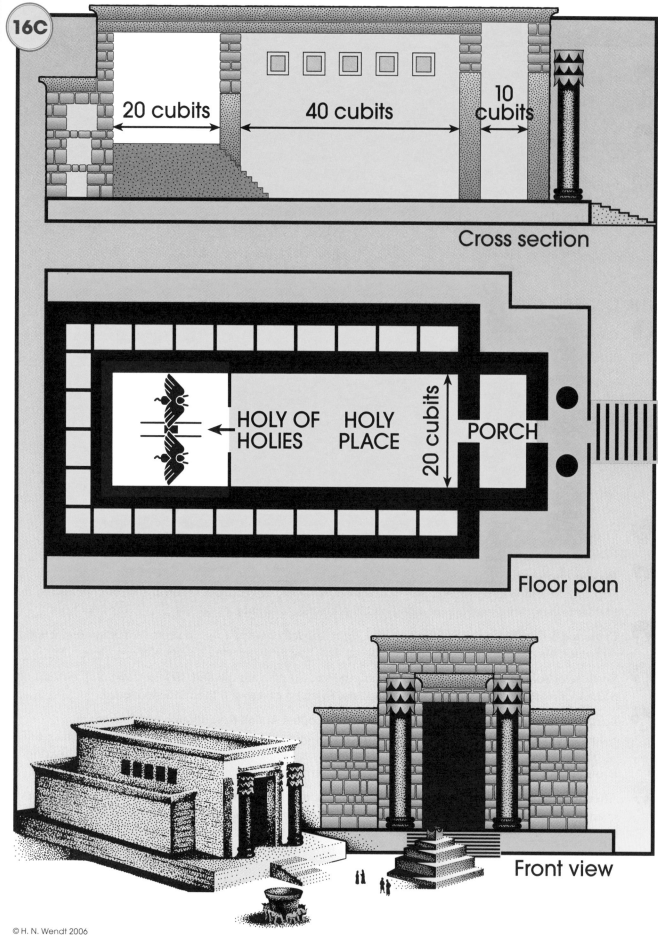

20 cubits

40 cubits

10 cubits

Cross section

HOLY OF HOLIES

HOLY PLACE

20 cubits

PORCH

Floor plan

Front view

1 Kings 6–8

1 Solomon's Temple was a rectangular building modeled after pagan temples but adapted for the worship of God. The building of the Temple is described in 1 Kings 6. **ILLUSTRATION 16C** gives its dimensions in cubits. A cubit is approximately 18" (45 cms)—roughly the distance between elbow and fingertips.

2 Two *free-standing bronze pillars* stood in front of the entrance *PORCH* or *vestibule*. They were named Jachin and Boaz, 7:15–22; their significance is not known.

3 The *HOLY OF HOLIES* was a cube and was kept in darkness. Its floor level was five cubits above the floor level of the Holy Place. It was separated from the larger *HOLY PLACE* by two doors of olive wood, 6:31,32 (according to 2 Chronicles 3:14, by a curtain—perhaps with reference to the postexilic Temple; in Herod's Temple, by a curtain, Luke 23:45). Only the High Priest could enter the Holy of Holies, which he did once each year on the Day of Atonement.

4 The Holy of Holies housed *two winged cherubim*, each fifteen feet (about 4.5 meters) high and with a fifteen foot wingspan. Their wings touched in the middle of the Holy of Holies and extended to the surrounding walls, 6:23–28. The *Ark of the Covenant* was placed in the center of the Holy of Holies under the wings of the cherubim, 8:6–8.

5 In the Holy Place were the *Golden Altar for Incense*, the *Table for the Bread of the Presence*, and *Ten Lamp-stands*, 7:48–50.

6 In front of the Temple stood the *Molten Sea* and the *Altar for Sacrifice*—the latter 20 cubits long, 20 cubits wide, and ten cubits high, 2 Chronicles 4:1. The Molten Sea was a huge bowl or tank supported by *twelve metal oxen*, 7:23–26. It was ten cubits in diameter and five cubits high. Its rim was about ten feet (3 meters) above ground level. According to 2 Chronicles 4:6, the priests used its waters for purification rituals when preparing themselves for service in the Temple.

7 It took seven years to build the Temple (6:38) and thirteen years to complete the rest of Solomon's building projects, including two palaces—one for Solomon and another for his Egyptian wife, 7:1–12. Ezekiel 43:6–9 suggests that Solomon's Temple was built close to his palace; if so, it might have served as a royal chapel.

8 1 Kings 7 states that, in addition to the Temple, Solomon built a *large complex* consisting of palaces and administrative offices. Some believe that many of Solomon's foreign wives served as political representatives of the nations from which they came, and that Solomon provided them with "office space" in the complex.

9 The meanings of some of the architectural terms used in relation to the Temple have been lost. However, 1 Kings states that a vast quantity of gold was used to adorn the interior of the Temple (6:20–22; 7:48–50), and that its walls and contents were decorated with symbols of cherubim, palm trees, open flowers, and lions, 6:18,29,32; 7:36.

10 To the *north*, *west*, and *south* of the Temple structure were *three-storey extensions*. It is not certain what function they served. Possibly they were storage rooms.

Throughout the narrative dealing with Solomon and the kings of Judah and Israel, it is important to keep in mind the message of 1 Kings 9:1–9. In 9:1–3, the Lord tells Solomon that His desire is to have His name, eyes, and heart dwell in the Jerusalem Temple "for all time." *If* Solomon and his successors walk as David walked, the dynasty will continue "forever," 9:4,5. But *if* they do not, the nation will lose the *Promised Land*, *Jerusalem*, the *Temple*, the *Davidic dynasty*, and its status as *God's people*, 9:6–9. The issue is: Will they worship *one God in one place*—as David did?

In this context, the message of Deuteronomy 17:14–20 is important. The passage states that after the people enter the Promised Land, they may indeed establish a line of kings. However, no king is to buy horses from Egypt, or seek to acquire many wives and great wealth. These "forbidden things" are the very things that Solomon did!

The Dedication of the Temple

1 1 Kings 8 describes the dedication of the Temple. After the Ark of the Covenant and other sacred vessels were installed in their appointed places, the cloud of the Lord's presence filled the Temple. The presence of the cloud symbolized God's approval of the structure, 8:1–11.

2 Solomon then addressed the assembly, 8:12–21. He began by saying that prior to the dedication of the Jerusalem Temple, God had not chosen any city in which to build a temple where His name would dwell, 8:16. (However, Jeremiah 7:12 states that, much earlier, God had chosen *Shiloh* as the place where His name should dwell "at first.") Furthermore, Solomon expanded greatly on the brief statement in 2 Samuel 7:13, "He (Solomon) shall build a *house* for my name." (It is possible that the term *house* in 2 Samuel 7:13 meant *line of kings*; Solomon would perpetuate David's dynasty.)

3 In 8:22–26, Solomon states that the Davidic dynasty will not come to an end *if David's successors walk as David walked*; note 8:25 and 1 Kings 2:4. In 1 and 2 Kings, this means that God's people must worship one God in Jerusalem as David did. The *if* is important. In 2 Samuel 7:13,15, David was told that his dynasty would last forever. Now the notion of David's dynasty coming to an end is declared a possibility.

4 A prayer of dedication follows, 8:22–53. After its opening remarks, it refers to the Davidic dynasty (see 2 Samuel 7:1–17) and then agonizes over precisely who or what resides in the Temple, 8:27–30. It suggests that God's *name* resides in the Temple, while His *presence* resides in heaven. Perhaps the point is: If one day the Temple is destroyed by a foreign power, that will not mean the end of God's existence. God's people, including those taken into exile in a foreign land, can still pray toward God's *presence* by facing toward *Jerusalem*.

5 A number of petitions follow that relate to:
- The settling of disputes, 8:31,32;
- Defeat in battle, 8:33,34;
- Drought, 8:35,36;
- Famine, pestilence, siege, sickness, 8:37–40;
- Gentile prayers, 8:41–43;
- Success in battle, 8:44,45;
- Life in exile, 8:46–53.

A significant detail appears in all of these petitions. Those who pray to God must do so facing the land of Israel, the city of Jerusalem, and the Temple, 8:30,33,35,38,42,44,48.

6 After praying, Solomon blesses the assembly and exhorts them to faithfulness, using Deuteronomic terms, 8:54–61. Solomon's words throughout ch. 8 give the impression that there is now a very close link between Jerusalem (and its Temple) and the Davidic dynasty.

7 Finally, a huge number of animals are sacrificed to the Lord—22,000 oxen and 120,000 sheep, 8:63. One might comment, "That's a lot of animals!"

8 In 9:1–9, God speaks some solemn words to Solomon. God begins by reminding Solomon of the promise to David that his dynasty would last forever, 2 Samuel 7:1–17; note 7:13,16 in particular. Then God says that *if* Solomon and his successors do not keep God's commandments and statutes, but serve and worship other gods, God will throw the people out of the land and destroy the Temple. There is no suggestion at this point that the Davidic dynasty might also come to an end.

When asked what they remember about Solomon, some say, "He built the Temple. He was wise. He had many wives." However, there was more to Solomon's reign than these three features.

1 Saul and David were anointed kings by the prophet Samuel, and the spirit of the Lord descended upon them in confirmation of that anointing, 1 Samuel 10:6,10; 16:13. There is no story of Solomon's anointing by the spirit nor any indication that the spirit of the Lord was with him. This remains true for all the kings who succeeded him. The spirit of the Lord is referred to in 1 and 2 Kings—but in relation to *prophets*, not *kings*. The important role played by the prophets in 1 and 2 Kings is underscored by the fact that they had the spirit of the Lord. Although kings ruled the people, it was the prophets who knew the Lord's will and spoke the Lord's word.

2 Some time after Solomon was made king, he divided the realm into administrative districts. He divided the northern section into 12 administrative districts (4:7), and left Judah as a unit under only one overseer, 4:19b. The army also played a key role, ensuring that the needs of the royal household and the Jerusalem politicians were met, 4:22,23,26,27. Although the more privileged looked on life in Solomon's day as "messianic" (4:20,25), others came to the conclusion that if there had to be kings, they should be as little like Solomon as possible, 1 Samuel 8:10–18; 1 Kings 12:4,14.

3 Solomon indulged in arms dealing; he imported horses and chariots from Cilicia and Egypt, and sold them to Hittite and Syrian kings, 10:29. Furthermore, when the time came for Solomon to pay the Phoenicians for their help with his building projects, he gave them twenty cities in Galilee, 9:10–14. Solomon *gave away part of the Promised Land*, apparently without asking the inhabitants how they felt about being given over to Phoenician rule. Apparently Hiram of Tyre was not impressed with the cities Solomon had handed over to him, 9:12,13. (The Chronicler, writing much later, could not live with this thought; he says that Hiram of Tyre gave cities to Solomon, 2 Chronicles 8:2.)

4 Solomon's material achievements were many. People came from afar to observe what life in Jerusalem was like during his reign, 10:1–10,24,25. Gold, silver, and cedar were common commodities in Solomon's day, 10:14–27. These external trimmings did not long survive after Solomon's death. Five years after he died, the Egyptians under Pharaoh Shishak plundered Judah and Jerusalem, stripped them of their gold and silver decorations and utensils, and carried the booty back to Egypt, 1 Kings 14:25–28.

5 Although we are told Solomon had a large harem, we are given details about only one of his wives, a (nameless) daughter of the Egyptian pharaoh, 3:1; 9:24. Possibly this marriage had value for political and trade relationships with Egypt, 10:28,29. The favored treatment extended to her would not have been without cost to his own people; he built a special palace for her, 7:8.

SOLOMON, THE WISE MAN

1 Solomon became the symbol for wisdom in subsequent Hebrew history. Portions of Proverbs are ascribed to him, as are also Ecclesiastes, the Song of Solomon, and the Wisdom of Solomon. 1 Kings 4:29–34 states that Solomon composed three thousand proverbs and a thousand and five songs. The apocryphal book of Ecclesiasticus (or Sirach) refers to Solomon in a negative manner (47:12–21), and includes him among those kings who abandoned the law of the Most High, 49:4.

2 It is possible that Solomon himself composed some wise sayings. Some scholars suggest that it is more likely that Solomon established an institution in which wisdom literature was produced. It was common practice in the world of his day, especially in Egypt, to have wise men attached to the king's court. If it was Solomon's ambition to establish an international reputation for himself, it would have been fitting for him to have a wisdom school. Writings produced in Solomon's wisdom school would have been ascribed to him and dedicated to him. Proverbs 25:1 indicates that Hezekiah had at his disposal men who worked with wisdom literature.

1 Although the writer would have been happy to report the details contained in 9:10–10:29 (*Solomon's splendor*), it would have pained him to write 11:1–12:33 (*Solomon's demise*).

2 In 11:3 we read that Solomon had 700 wives and 300 concubines. This statistic did not trouble the writer. What troubled him was the fact that many of them were foreign women who eventually misled Solomon into the worship of their false gods, 11:1,2,4–8.

3 While reporting these details, the writer states that because Solomon built shrines for the worship of these false gods, his heart was not wholly true to the Lord his God as was the heart of David his father, 11:4,6. David worshiped *one God in one place*; Solomon did not.

4 What does the writer mean when he states that David's heart was true to the Lord his God, and that he completely followed the Lord? The meaning is: David worshipped *one God in one place*—and by the writer's time that place is not merely *Jerusalem*, but the *Temple in Jerusalem*. The issue throughout is *monotheism* in the Jerusalem Temple versus *polytheism* everywhere else—in other words, worshiping *one God in one place* as opposed to worshiping *many gods in many places*.

5 In 11:9–13, the writer explains what must happen as a result of Solomon's polytheism. David's descendants would not rule David's extensive realm, but only Judah. A major part of David's empire would be lost. Even so, Judah and Jerusalem must continue so that David's descendants will have a place from which to rule, and that those remaining in Judah can continue to worship God in the Jerusalem Temple.

6 The nation began to crumble during Solomon's reign. The *Edomites* (11:14–22) broke away, and the *Syrians* did the same, 11:23–25.

7 A significant event follows, 11:26–40. When Jeroboam (the head of forced labor in the northern region) left Jerusalem, he was met by a prophet, Ahijah the Shilonite. Ahijah tore his new outer garment into twelve pieces, gave ten pieces to Jeroboam, and assured him that the kingdom would be split into two parts after Solomon's death. Jeroboam would then rule the ten northern tribes. Judah (and Benjamin, 12:21) would continue under Solomon's son. The reason for the coming division was Solomon's idolatry.

God would permit Judah and Jerusalem to continue under Solomon's son, Rehoboam, for the sake of David, who kept God's commandments and statutes, 11:33,34. Furthermore, Ahijah assured Jeroboam that:

- *if* he listened to all that God commanded him,
- *if* he walked in God's ways,
- *if* he did what was right in God's sight by keeping His statutes and commandments (as David had done),

… Jeroboam's dynasty would endure, and God would be with him, 11:38. Ahijah's statement is significant. He was saying that if Jeroboam continued to worship "one God in the Jerusalem Temple" (as David had done) he and his descendants would continue to rule the soon-to-be kingdom of Israel. Dynastic stability is linked to Deuteronomic religiosity—"*one God in one place*."

8 Until this point, there is no suggestion that the Davidic dynasty would *actually* come to an end. Yes, the *one* kingdom would become *two*. But Judah and Jerusalem would continue, so that the Davidic dynasty might rule from there, 11:36,39.

9 When Solomon heard about Jeroboam's future role, he plotted to kill him. To preserve his life, Jeroboam fled to Egypt, 11:40. Eventually Solomon died, 11:41–43.

10 After Solomon's death, his son Rehoboam went to Shechem to try to persuade those living in the northern part of the realm to accept him as their king. However, the northerners revolted and made Jeroboam their king, 12:1–24. Without doubt, the northerners' plea was justified (12:4), the advice of Rehoboam's older advisers was sound (12:6,7), the advice of Rehoboam's young friends stupid (12:10,11), and Rehoboam's decision irresponsible, 12:12–15. The nation split!

 Solomon's exploitation of his people had resulted in an event that Isaiah (7:17) declared to be the greatest disaster in the history of the nation—the division of the Kingdom.

 That Judah accepted Rehoboam's rule without question is understandable. The newly ornamented Jerusalem was basically a southern city which the southerners could look upon as their show piece. Furthermore, Jerusalem's grandeur had been achieved at a price—the sweat of many northerners!

JEROBOAM'S "SIN"

1 Kings 12:25–33

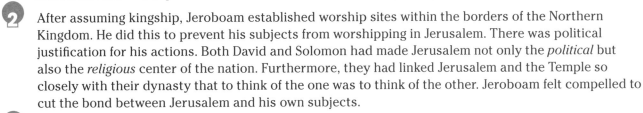

1 After Jeroboam was made king of the Northern Kingdom, he first established a seat of government at Shechem. Later his capital was moved to Penuel in the Transjordan, 12:25.

2 After assuming kingship, Jeroboam established worship sites within the borders of the Northern Kingdom. He did this to prevent his subjects from worshipping in Jerusalem. There was political justification for his actions. Both David and Solomon had made Jerusalem not only the *political* but also the *religious* center of the nation. Furthermore, they had linked Jerusalem and the Temple so closely with their dynasty that to think of the one was to think of the other. Jeroboam felt compelled to cut the bond between Jerusalem and his own subjects.

3 Although Jeroboam did not reestablish Shiloh as a worship site within his realm, he did establish shrines in Bethel and Dan.
- *Bethel* lay just to the north of the border between Israel and Judah. Why go to Jerusalem when there was a nearby worship site within Israel's borders?
- *Dan* was at the northern edge of the new kingdom and would cater to the needs of Jeroboam's subjects living in its vicinity. The origins of Dan as a shrine locality are given in Judges 17,18. This shrine still functioned at the time of Amos (Amos 8:14).

4 Jeroboam installed a golden calf in each of these shrines. Most likely, these were initially not meant to be images of God, but were to serve as symbols of God's presence. If they had been designed to serve as images of God, the prophets would have attacked them. But neither Elijah nor Elisha said a word against them—nor did Amos. And when eventually Jehu purged Baal worship from Israel, he did not remove Jeroboam's "calves," 2 Kings 10:28–31. There is reason to believe that the problem the writer of Kings had with Jeroboam's shrines was not so much their *theology* as their *geography*.

5 Because the bull symbolized the Canaanite god, Baal, Jeroboam's actions might have resulted in northern worshipers confusing the Lord with Baal.

6 1 Kings 12:32 makes reference to a feast—most likely the Feast of Tabernacles. Its celebration at Bethel would have lured northerners there rather than going to Jerusalem to celebrate it. The writer views with displeasure not only Jeroboam's shrines but also his ecclesiastical calendar and non-Levite priests, 12:31,32; 13:33,34. Although Judges 18:30,31 links the lineage of the priests at Dan to Moses, 2 Kings 23:15–20 describes their eventual slaughter with delight.

7 As a result of King Josiah's reform (2 Kings 22,23; to be studied in Unit 19), Jerusalem became the only legitimate shrine in the realm. Josiah's reform took place in 621 B.C. The writer of 1 and 2 Kings finished his work sometime after 560 B.C. (see 2 Kings 25:27–30 where reference is made to Jehoiachin being freed from prison in Babylon in 560 B.C.); he dismissed any shrine outside Jerusalem as a "high place." Although this term is normally associated with a pagan altar, the writer of Kings uses it in the sense of being "invalid" (because sacrifice should be offered only in the Jerusalem Temple). Furthermore, the northern shrines would have been particularly abhorrent to the writer, for in his mind they contributed greatly to the collapse of the nation. Worship at those shrines resulted in the neglect of the Jerusalem Temple, and therefore in the neglect of God. He attacks them, and any shrine apart from the Temple, throughout his account.

16A After succeeding his father David, Solomon had his brother Adonijah killed, and the priest Abiathar exiled; they had posed a threat in his bid for the throne. He also had Joab (his cousin) and Shimei (a Benjaminite) executed—which David had commanded him to do.

Solomon did away with the borders of the former Tribal League, and placed 12 officials over the northern part of his realm and one over Judah. He also married many foreign women—perhaps with a view to cementing relations with their countries of origin. Solomon undertook extensive building ventures both within and beyond Jerusalem, including a harbor city at Ezion-geber and fortresses at Hazor, Megiddo, and Gezer.

During the early part of his reign, some were loud in their praises with regard to life under Solomon. They rejoiced that the nation had a large population, and that all were able to eat, drink, and be happy!

16B However, with the passing of time opinions changed. Not only had Solomon married many foreign women; he had also built shrines for the worship of the false gods his wives and concubines had brought with them. Furthermore, he made use of forced labor to carry out his building ventures. Toward the close of Solomon's reign, the Syrians and Edomites revolted against Solomon and gained their independence. Already prior to Solomon's death, a prophet predicted that the nation would eventually split into two regions.

16C The best known of Solomon's building projects was the Jerusalem Temple—an ornate and lavish structure that played an important role in the history of God's people until it was destroyed by the Babylonians in 587 B.C.

16D Solomon himself presided at the dedication of the Temple—during the course of which he had the Ark of the Covenant placed in the structure's Holy of Holies. The Temple had taken seven years to build. In the prayer of dedication, Solomon encouraged the people to pray about many needs and challenges—but always to face the Temple while doing so, even when in exile in a distant land.

16E Although the spirit of God comes upon both Saul and David, no reference is made to the spirit of God coming upon Solomon. Solomon certainly ensured that his personal needs, and those of his household, were met. To pay the Phoenicians for their role in his building projects, Solomon gave them part of the Promised Land—20 cities in Galilee! He also engaged in the sale of weapons; he bought horses and chariots from Egypt and sold them to nations to the north of his realm.

Although tradition ascribes to Solomon the writing of much wisdom literature, it is possible that—in keeping with Ancient Near Eastern practices—he made use of "wise men" in his court to produce these. Because Solomon had funded these writing projects, the end result was attributed to him.

16F Although Israel progressed materially as a result of Solomon's efforts, its spiritual strength diminished. Solomon's negative example contributed toward this state of affairs. After his death, the citizens of the northern regions made it clear to Solomon's son and successor, Rehoboam, that they had no intention of submitting to his rule as a matter of course. They wanted a satisfactory policy statement before making any commitment. When Rehoboam told the northerners that he would rule them even more harshly than his father had done, the northerners declared their independence from Judah and appointed Jeroboam—a former overseer of Solomon's forced labor projects—as their king. What had been a United Kingdom now became a divided kingdom.

After being made king of the Northern Kingdom, Jeroboam established shrines at Bethel and Dan, placed a golden calf in each, and appointed priests of his own choosing to serve at them. The purpose of these shrines was to prevent his subjects from having any further contact with Judah, Jerusalem and its Temple, and the Davidic dynasty.

UNITS 11–20

From the Conquest to the Babylonian Exile

UNIT 17
From Two to One

The Histories of Judah and Israel
from the Division to the Assyrian Destruction of Israel in 721 B.C.

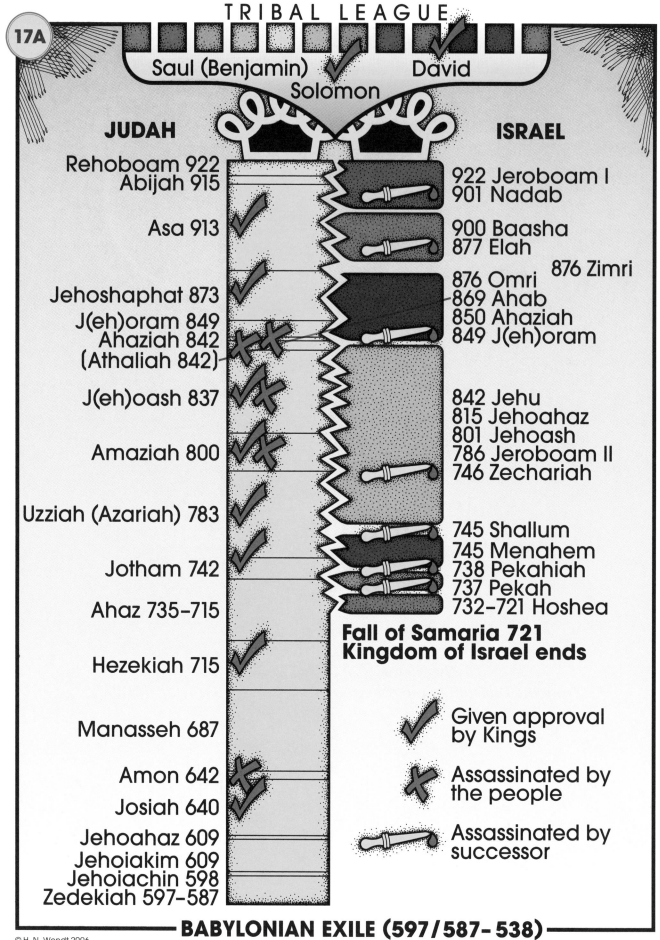

TRIBAL LEAGUE

Saul (Benjamin)   David
Solomon

JUDAH   **ISRAEL**

Rehoboam 922   922 Jeroboam I
Abijah 915   901 Nadab

Asa 913   900 Baasha
                                        877 Elah

                                        876 Omri   876 Zimri
Jehoshaphat 873   869 Ahab
J(eh)oram 849   850 Ahaziah
Ahaziah 842   849 J(eh)oram
(Athaliah 842)

J(eh)oash 837   842 Jehu
                                        815 Jehoahaz
                                        801 Jehoash
Amaziah 800   786 Jeroboam II
                                        746 Zechariah

Uzziah (Azariah) 783
                                        745 Shallum
                                        745 Menahem
Jotham 742   738 Pekahiah
                                        737 Pekah
Ahaz 735–715   732–721 Hoshea

Fall of Samaria 721
Kingdom of Israel ends

Hezekiah 715

Manasseh 687   ✔ Given approval
                                          by Kings

Amon 642   ✗ Assassinated by
                                          the people
Josiah 640

Jehoahaz 609   Assassinated by
Jehoiakim 609   successor
Jehoiachin 598
Zedekiah 597–587

BABYLONIAN EXILE (597/587–538)

ILLUSTRATION 17A is an overview of the histories of Judah and Israel. It lists the kings who ruled:

- *The United Kingdom* (**Saul**, **David**, **Solomon**): Just how united the kingdom was during this period is debatable.
- *The Southern Kingdom* (**JUDAH**): 19 kings, plus the upstart Queen **Athaliah**, daughter of the northern king, **Ahab**, and his Phoenician wife, Jezebel. Athaliah ruled Judah for about six years, 2 Kings 11:1–21; see v. 1–3. (Note the **line linking Athaliah to her father, Ahab of ISRAEL**.)
- *The Northern Kingdom* (**ISRAEL**): 19 kings.

It is virtually impossible to determine accurately the length of the reign of most of the kings listed in **ILLUSTRATION 17A**.

 **The United Kingdom**

   a. How long **Saul** reigned is uncertain, 1 Samuel 13:1. His son, Ish-bosheth, ruled for several years, 2 Samuel 2:10,11.

   b. **David** ruled Judah for seven years, and then the United Kingdom for 33 years.

   c. **Solomon** ruled the United Kingdom for 40 years.

The Divided Kingdom—JUDAH, the Southern Kingdom

   a. One dynasty, David and his descendants, ruled in Judah (with one exception: Queen **Athaliah**, a northern princess who married Jehoram, see 2 Kings 11).

   b. The continuing Davidic dynasty contributed toward political stability in Judah, and (very likely) to the fact that the southern realm survived longer than its northern neighbor.

   c. 1 and 2 Kings either commend or condemn each king on the basis of the attitude he adopted toward Jerusalem and its Temple. They *disapprove* of all northern kings because they encouraged worship at shrines other than the Jerusalem Temple, 1 Kings 12:25–33. They *approve* of some southern kings because they repaired the Jerusalem Temple or reformed the worship life practiced within it, 1 Kings 3:1–3; 11:4–8; 2 Kings 18:1–8 (Hezekiah); 22:2, 23:25 (Josiah).

   d. Although five kings of Judah were assassinated, no change in dynasty took place. **Ahaziah** of Judah was killed by **Jehu** of Israel. The other four assassinations were carried out by people from within Judah. In each case, a legitimate descendant of David was placed on the throne to succeed the person assassinated.

   e. *The Babylonians took exiles from Judah to Babylon in **597** B.C.* (including 18 year-old King Jehoiachin) and again in **587** B.C. (including King **Zedekiah**, whom they blinded after forcing him to watch his sons being executed, 2 Kings 24:10–12; ch. 25).

The Divided Kingdom—ISRAEL, the Northern Kingdom

   a. Nine dynasties ruled Israel; four of these consisted of only one ruler (**Zimri**, **Shallum**, **Pekah**, **Hoshea**). Zimri committed suicide after ruling for seven days (1 Kings 16:8–20), and Shallum reigned for only one month, 2 Kings 15:8–15; neither is assigned a **color block** in the *illustration* (the **seven color blocks** refer to the other seven dynasties).

   b. In seven cases, dynastic change was brought about by assassination (**daggers**).

   c. *The Assyrians destroyed Israel in **721** B.C.*

Kings: To continue or not to continue?

According to 2 Kings 25:27–30, **Jehoiachin** of Judah was still alive in Babylon in 560 B.C. There was hope that he would live through the exile, return to Judah and Jerusalem, and reestablish the Davidic dynasty. However, he did not return and died in Babylon. To understand this is to begin to understand the significance of Matthew 1:1 (especially in the NRSV translation) which states that Jesus was a descendant of David! In Jesus the Messiah, the Davidic dynasty was being restored—but in a form very different from what the people were expecting! **Jesus, David's Final Descendant, washed feet and calls His followers to do the same**, John 13:1–17, 31–35.

After the division of the realm, the Southern Kingdom resumed using its old name of Judah and the Northern Kingdom was known as Israel. Each kingdom thought of itself as the chosen nation and the true people of God. The two kingdoms were different in numerous ways.

1. *Judah's* lower rainfall and less fertile soil often made it difficult for the people to produce sufficient food to meet their needs. Geographically, Judah was more removed from other nations and therefore less subject to influence by them. Many in Judah adhered to the simple lifestyles of nomad and shepherd—occupations which kept at arm's length the temptations associated with the settled life of farmer and town-dweller.

2. *Israel's* soil was more fertile than Judah's, and therefore able to produce better cattle and more abundant grain and fruit crops. Furthermore, Israel's geographical position made it easier to have active trade links with nearby countries such as Phoenicia. At the same time, Israel's location made the nation more vulnerable to influence from outside sources, particularly religious practices.

THE INTERNATIONAL SCENE

1. The history of the people of God took place in the rough-and-tumble of international history. About the time Israel and Judah were establishing themselves as kingdoms, Egypt and Assyria were flexing their muscles and adding neighboring territories to their own.

2. Egypt had kept to itself during the reigns of Saul, David, and Solomon. Things changed when a Libyan prince called Sheshonk (Shishak in the Bible) conquered Egypt and established the twenty-second Egyptian dynasty. He invaded Israel and Judah about five years after Solomon's death, 1 Kings 14:25–28. Sheshonk was apparently content with the plunder obtained from this campaign, for he made no attempt to set up any political control over either realm. The Egyptians did not involve themselves in the wider history of the world beyond that time, possibly because they had trouble dealing with intrusions first by the Ethiopians and then by the Assyrians.

3. The people of Israel and Judah had good reasons to fear the Assyrians. First, the Assyrians were developing an appetite for empire. Second, they were a fiercely cruel people who impaled their enemies or burned them alive, tore people apart limb by limb, built pyramids out of human skulls, and decorated their furnishings and the walls of their homes with human skin. Tiglath-Pileser (1114–1076 B.C.) pushed Assyria's borders westward to the shores of the Mediterranean and left it at that. Later Assyrian rulers sent their military machines into more southern areas. Although Assyria's growth was slow and gradual, during the years following the division of the United Kingdom into Judah and Israel, Assyria was a force to be feared.

4. There were other political threats. The Philistines continued to covet Judah and Israel. Furthermore, the Syrians had plans for the region. Further south were the Edomites and Moabites. However, for several centuries Assyria remained Public Enemy Number One.

The details recorded in 1 and 2 Kings were not written by an eyewitness. The last verses in 2 Kings indicate that the work was completed some time after 560 B.C. (See 2 Kings 25:27–30. Nebuchadnezzar took Jehoiachin into exile in Babylon in 597 B.C.; the 37th year of Jehoiachin's exile was 560 B.C.) The author does not give a detailed account of all that transpired in the life of each king. He refers those wishing to have more information about the reign of each king to *The Book of the Chronicles of the Kings of Israel* and *The Book of the Chronicles of the Kings of Judah* (not the canonical 1 and 2 Chronicles). His major themes are:

1 The histories of the kings of Judah and Israel are outlined from Deuteronomy's viewpoint: God blesses those who are obedient to Him, and punishes those who disobey Him. People must love the Lord with all their heart, soul, and strength, and never worship other gods, Deuteronomy 6:4,5.

2 Worship must be centered in Jerusalem. Worship at other sanctuaries, referred to as "high places," exposed the nation to religious contamination. 1 and 2 Kings reflect the influence of Josiah's reform which took place in 621 B.C., 2 Kings 22,23. (This reform will be studied in Unit 19.) The writer assumes that it had always been the will of God that all worship be centered in Jerusalem, and that Jerusalem had always been the city in which God made His name to dwell. (See 1 Kings 8:16; 9;3; 14:21. Note also Jeremiah 7:12 where the prophet states that God first chose Shiloh as the place where His name would dwell.) Other shrines are referred to as high places, even though they were not necessarily idolatrous. For example, before Solomon built the Temple in Jerusalem, he worshipped at Gibeon—referred to as the "great high place," even though the Lord appeared to Solomon there, 1 Kings 3:3–9.

3 The writer has a specific purpose in mind—which will become more obvious when Unit 19 is studied. However, the following advance comments will help:

    a. It is very likely that 1 Kings 1:1–2 Kings 23:25 was completed during the reign of Josiah, some time after 621 B.C. 2 Kings 23:5 states:

        Before Josiah there was no king like him, who turned to the Lord with all his heart, with all his soul, with all his might, according to all the law of Moses; nor did any like him arise after him.

    b. However, precisely the same comment was made concerning Hezekiah (2 Kings 18:5) who reigned 715–687 B.C. According to 2 Kings 18:1–7 and Isaiah 36:7, Hezekiah attempted to free Judah from Assyrian control and centralize all worship in Jerusalem. Apparently he did not succeed.

    c. Josiah succeeded in doing what Hezekiah had failed to do. He put an end to the worship of the heavenly bodies (astral deities worshiped by the Assyrians) and destroyed altars built by Ahaz and Manasseh—all symbols of submission to Assyria, 2 Kings 23:4,5,12. He established control over the former Northern Kingdom (23:15–20) and centralized all worship in Jerusalem, 23:21–23.

    d. The writer's point is: Josiah gave back to Judah and Israel the "good old days of David"— a united realm that worshipped *one God in one place* (Jerusalem), and was ruled from Jerusalem by a king from the Davidic line.

4 However, in 609 B.C. Josiah was killed by the Egyptians at Megiddo when he tried to stop their march north to prop up Assyria as a buffer against the emerging Babylonian threat. With Josiah's death, the dream of the restoration of "the days of David" died! So the author of 1 and 2 Kings finishes his writing project in Babylon, merely cataloging the reigns of Josiah's three sons and one grandson without comparing their reigns to that of David.

5 In completing the writing project, the author offers insights about why the nation had been brought to ruin. God was behind the disaster! God was punishing the people because they had ignored the warnings of the prophets and had committed all kinds of faithless deeds, 2 Kings 17:7–18. They had run after other gods and had not worshipped *one God in one place*, the Jerusalem Temple. His account is not solely negative—listing past sins. It is optimistic and full of hope as well. After all, Jehoiachin is still alive and hopefully will go back to Jerusalem to reestablish the Davidic dynasty there. And hopefully, the nation itself will eventually go back. If the nation takes God and the Sinai covenant seriously, it can look forward to a happy future. However, it must, like David and Josiah, worship *one God in one place*—the Jerusalem Temple!

6 Kings contains much information about the work of the prophets. The writer devotes most of 1 Kings 17–2 Kings 10 to describing the work and influence of *Elijah* and *Elisha*. These two prophetic giants devoted their energies to the destruction of Baal worship and to proclaiming the word of the Lord. The villain throughout 1 Kings 17–22 is Ahab, for during his reign the faith of Israel was locked in mortal combat with Baal worship. After Elijah's ascension (2 Kings 2), Elisha continued in similar style against the same enemy. Most of 2 Kings 4:1–8:6 is devoted to a description of Elisha's miracles.

Other prophets appear on the scene as well: *Ahijah* (1 Kings 14:4); *an unnamed prophet*, 1 Kings 20:13,28,35; *Micaiah*, 1 Kings 22:8–28. Frequent reference is made to the "sons of the prophets," 2 Kings 2:3,5; 4:1; 5:22; 6:1; 9:1–13. Reference is also made to prophets more concerned about their job security than proclaiming God's truth, 1 Kings 22:5–12.

7 The word the Lord's prophets proclaimed was more than eloquent oratory. It was the vehicle through which the Lord's power shaped and directed the course of history, 1 Kings 19:15–18; 2 Kings 9,10. Not only did God use the prophets to direct the history of the kings and people, but God also placed them within the royal court to advise the king personally, 2 Kings 6:12,21; 13:14–19.

The prophets did not base what they proclaimed on personal whims. They were men of the covenant. The God they proclaimed was the God of the Exodus—the jealous God who tolerates no rivals. To ignore God was to invite destruction.

8 Accounts of war are woven into the entire narrative in 1 and 2 Kings. Israel or Judah, either together or separately, are repeatedly fighting one of their neighbors, or, worse yet, one another, 1 Kings 14:30; 15:7; 2 Kings 14:8–14.

The history of each king of Judah and Israel is set within a literary framework:

1 JUDAH, the Southern Kingdom

   a. *In the _____ year of _____, king of Israel, _____, king of Judah began to reign.*

   b. *Details about his age, length of reign, name, and queen mother are given.*

   c. *The king's reign is evaluated in comparison to that of "David his father."*

   d. *"Now the rest of the acts of _____, are they not written in the Book of the Chronicles of the Kings of Judah?"*

   e. *"He slept with his fathers, and _____ reigned in his stead."*

A limited number of southern kings receive any approval. Only three southern kings (David, Hezekiah, and Josiah) are given whole-hearted approval. Ten southern rulers fail the test miserably, for "they did what was evil in the sight of the Lord." When one becomes aware that the yardstick used to measure the worth of a king is the attitude he adopted toward worship in Jerusalem, one becomes more conscious of the fact that the record in Kings focuses more on the Temple than on the person of the king. Note the description of Joash's reign, 2 Kings 12; although he reigned for forty years (12:1), Kings focuses largely on how the Temple fared during his reign.

2 ISRAEL, the Northern Kingdom

   a. *In the _____ year of _____, king of Judah, _____, king of Israel, began to reign.*

   b. *Details are given about the length of his reign and the place of his capital.*

   c. *He is castigated in that "he did what was evil in the sight of the Lord, and walked in the way of Jeroboam and his sin which he made Israel to sin."*

   d. *"Now the rest of the acts of _____, are they not written in the Book of the Chronicles of the Kings of Israel?"*

   e. *"He slept with his fathers, and _____ reigned in his stead."*

Every northern king is judged to have been evil. With almost monotonous regularity the comment is made of each northern king, "He did what was evil in the sight of the Lord; he did not depart all his days from any of the sins of Jeroboam the son of Nebat, which he caused Israel to sin," 2 Kings 15:18. As Unit 16 pointed out, Jeroboam's sin was that he encouraged and allowed worship at shrines other than the Jerusalem Temple, placed a golden calf in each one, installed priests of questionable legitimacy, and set up his own calendar of religious festivals.

1 Nine dynasties played a role in the history of the Northern Kingdom. Only two of these lasted more than two generations. In seven cases the takeover of one dynasty from another was achieved through assassination. The one exception was the emergence of Omri's dynasty, for Zimri committed suicide after only seven days on the throne, 1 Kings 16:15–20. Assassinations also took place in the south. However, these assassinations were not carried out by a candidate for the throne but by power groups within the nation seeking to replace an undesirable king with his more acceptable son; see **ILLUSTRATION 17A** and 2 Kings 12:20; 14:19.

2 Judah enjoyed more dynastic stability than did Israel. Why? All southern kings (with the exception of Queen Athaliah, a daughter of Ahab and Jezebel) came from the line of David, and Jerusalem provided Judah with a secure political and religious center. Some kings of Judah reigned for long periods, e.g., Asa for 41 years and Jehoshaphat for 25 years.

3 On the other hand, during the period 913–850 B.C., no less than seven northern kings followed one another:

- Jeroboam I was followed by his son…
- Nadab, who was assassinated two years later by…
- Baasha, who was succeeded by his son…
- Elah, who was murdered by…
- Zimri, who committed suicide after seven days and was followed by…
- Omri, who was succeeded by his son…
- Ahab.

4 The last years of Israel's history were chaotic. Jeroboam II died in 746 B.C. The Assyrians captured the land and led thousands of its leading citizens into exile in 721 B.C. During the intervening 25 years, six kings sat on the throne of Israel. In four instances, the new monarch gained the throne by assassinating the incumbent!

Different forms of kingship prevailed in the Ancient Near East. In Egypt, the pharaoh was thought to be divine. In Mesopotamia, the king was an "adopted" son of the national god. It was believed that the order of the cosmos itself was linked to the nature of a king's rule. The king was also to maintain order in society by defending the nation and upholding justice. Priesthood and kingship went hand in hand, and the role of the king was absolute.

In Israel, the king was viewed as God's "adopted" son, Psalm 2:7. Israel's kings were in charge of the military and were to uphold justice. Deuteronomy 17:14–20 defines the divine intention with regard to kingship. The king is to fear God and keep the commandments. The king does not have absolute power, but is to rule according to the law of Moses. Then and only then will there be peace and prosperity in the nation. In 1 and 2 Kings the focus of the events reported is whether or not the kings lived in accordance with the law, especially with regard to the centralization of worship in Jerusalem.

First and Second Kings devote considerable space to the ministries of *Elijah* and *Elisha*. Their primary function was to speak the word of the Lord to the king and his people, to indict both king and people for their failure to live according to the commandments, and to warn of coming judgment with the hope that both king and people would repent. According to Deuteronomy 18:15–22, the validity of a prophet's message was established by its fulfillment. The words of Elijah and Elisha were fulfilled repeatedly. Although both performed wonders, their exhortations to worship the Lord, and the Lord alone, were more important, Deuteronomy 13.

A brief summary of the ministries of Elijah and Elisha

1 *Elijah and the drought* (1 Kings 17:1–6)
Elijah appears unannounced and says there will be no rain except by the word he speaks on God's behalf. The Lord cares for Elijah during the drought.

2 *The widow's last meal* (1 Kings 17:7–16)
The Lord's care now extends to a widow who shares her last meal with Elijah.

3 *Elijah and the widow's son* (1 Kings 17:17–24)
A widow's son becomes ill. God responds to Elijah's prayer and restores the son to health.

4 *Elijah and the prophets of Baal* (1 Kings 18)
The question at stake in the confrontation between Elijah and the prophets of Baal is: Who controls fertility in the land, Baal or God? The incident shows that God is not only a Warrior-God who can rescue the Israelites from Egypt, but also the God who controls nature in Canaan and provides for the physical needs of the Israelites.

5 *Elijah on Mt. Horeb/Sinai* (1 Kings 19:1–18)
There are parallels between this narrative and the Exodus tradition. Furthermore, God can reveal His presence in the most unexpected ways, even in a still small voice. God has not deserted the Israelites, but continues to direct their history. God also directs the history of their neighbors, for Elijah is to anoint Hazael as king of Syria. Elijah is commanded to anoint Elisha and Jehu for specific tasks within Israel. Despite the inroads Baal worship was making into Israel's worship life, some had remained faithful to God and a remnant would be preserved. Elijah eventually appoints Elisha, and the other commands are carried out by other prophets.

6 *Elisha is called* (1 Kings 19:19–21)
Elijah throws his cloak over Elisha—signifying a transfer of power.

7 *Elijah, Ahab, and Naboth's vineyard* (1 Kings 21)
In Israel, land belonged to the Lord and could not be sold at will. Ahab and Jezebel set themselves

above the law of the Lord with total disregard for their subjects, and contrive to purchase Naboth's vineyard. Elijah condemns Ahab and Jezebel, and says that the house of Ahab will be annihilated. Because Ahab repents, the punishment is deferred to his son.

8 *Elijah transfers authority to Elisha* (2 Kings 2:1–18)
Although the story contains unique details, the point is that Elisha is Elijah's true successor. He walks in Elijah's footsteps, divides the waters of the Jordan, and God's spirit dwells within him.

9 *Elisha and the bitter waters* (2 Kings 2:19–22)
In purifying bitter waters, Elisha shows that he has been endowed with God's power and is Elijah's rightful successor.

10 *Elisha and the boys of Bethel* (2 Kings 2:23–25)
When some boys call Elisha names, they are killed by bears. Although the consequence seems out of balance with the cause, the story shows the power of the prophet in relation to curse as well as blessing.

11 *Elisha and the campaign against Moab* (2 Kings 3:4–27)
When the kings of Israel, Judah, and Edom go to war with Moab, they consult Elisha concerning water supplies for their armies. Elisha uses music to make himself receptive to God's spirit, and then assures the kings that God will supply them with water and grant them victory over the Moabites.

12 *Elisha and the widow's oil* (2 Kings 4:1–7)
The story reflects Elijah's action in Kings 17:17–24. In both incidents, God provides the needy with an unfailing supply.

13 *Elisha and the Shunammite woman's son* (2 Kings 4:8–37)
Elisha's actions reflect those of Elijah in 1 Kings 17:17–24. Life and blessing come from God through God's prophets. Although Elisha's servant, Gehazi, cannot help the boy, his master can.

14 *Elisha and the poisoned stew* (2 Kings 4:38–41)
The story reveals Elisha's authority, and the power of his prayers on behalf of his followers.

15 *Elisha multiplies loaves of bread* (2 Kings 4:42–44)
The Canaanites thought that Baal, the god of fertility, provided bread for the people. Elisha's actions point to God as the provider of food.

16 *Elisha cures Naaman of leprosy* (2 Kings 5:1–27)
After Elisha heals him of leprosy, Naaman recognizes the God of Israel as the source of all healing and the only God in all the earth—a remarkable confession from a pagan. The greed and deception of Gehazi, Elisha's servant, result in appropriate punishment for him. Elisha wanted to share God's blessing with Naaman; Gehazi wanted money for himself.

17 *Elisha and the floating axe-head* (2 Kings 6:1–7)
Elisha uses God-given powers to help one of his followers.

18 *Elisha and the Syrian siege* (2 Kings 6:8–7:20)
The narrative begins with Elisha enabling the king of Israel to thwart Syrian attempts to penetrate Israel. Those whom the Syrian king sent to capture Elisha at Dothan are smitten with blindness, then healed and fed, and sent back to Syria. When Ben-hadad of Syria sets siege to Samaria, people within the city suffer severely from lack of food and blame Elisha for their situation. Finally, the Syrian army flees before a few lepers looking for food. Once again the word of the Lord, spoken by a true prophet, is fulfilled.

 The Shunammite woman obeys Elisha (2 Kings 8:1–6)

The story is a continuation of that in 4:8–37. In keeping with Elisha's advice the woman had left her country, lost claim to her husband's land, and was without means of support. She is helped by the king who acts because of Elisha's reputation.

Elisha, Hazael, and the death of Ben-hadad (2 Kings 8:7–15)

When Ben-hadad seeks an oracle of recovery, Elisha announces both his recovery and death. Only the latter is fulfilled. Elisha is shown to have knowledge of the future.

Two other incidents involving prophets occur in 1 Kings:

- *Ahab and an unnamed prophet* (1 Kings 20)

   An unnamed prophet advises Ahab on how to cope with incursions and harassments by Ben-hadad of Syria. After Ahab finally achieves victory, the prophet rebukes him for failing to carry out the rules of Holy War in relation to Ben-hadad. Ahab should have killed Ben-hadad, not spared him.

- *Ahab and Micaiah* (1 Kings 22)

   The unnamed prophet of 1 Kings 20 had condemned Ahab to death. In 1 Kings 21:17–29, Elijah tells Ahab that his dynasty will be wiped out as had previous northern dynasties, and that Jezebel will be eaten by dogs. Although Ahab would not be the last member of the dynasty, his son would.

   In 1 Kings 22, Ahab of Israel and Jehoshaphat of Judah join forces to recover Ramoth-gilead from Syrian control. Ahab first consults court prophets concerning the outcome of the approaching battle. They are more than ready to tell the king what he wants to hear. One of their number, Zedekiah, even uses a symbolic act to deliver his message, 2:11. Eventually Ahab asks Micaiah for his opinion about the outcome. Micaiah predicts that Ahab will lose the battle and be killed. Subsequent events prove Micaiah to be right.

1 Kings 12–2 Kings 17

The information below is complex. It provides a brief overview of the period under review. Because the writer of 1 and 2 Kings records and interprets history through the lens of the central themes in Deuteronomy (e.g., *one God in one place*), he will be referred to as the *Deuteronomist*.

The background colors within the charts denote separate dynasties and reflect the dynastic divisions depicted in **ILLUSTRATION 17A**. Note that the succession of kings within Judah came from the same dynasty throughout that nation's history—with the brief exception of Queen Athaliah's reign.

JUDAH JUDAH JUDAH JUDAH

Rehoboam 922–915

The Deuteronomist does not evaluate Rehoboam. Instead he evaluates the people of Judah. Because the people worshiped at local shrines and incorporated pagan beliefs and practices into their worship forms, they were guilty of apostasy. Five years after Solomon's death, Pharaoh Sheshonk of Egypt sent a military expedition from Egypt through Palestine and Syria. Among other things, the Egyptians looted the Jerusalem Temple—an action that is seen as divine punishment for the failure of the people to worship the Lord, and the Lord alone. (1 Kings 14:21–31)

Abijah (or Abijam) 915–913

Rehoboam was followed by his son, Abijah. Like his father, Abijah engaged in warfare with his northern neighbor. Although he is viewed with disfavor, God allowed his son, Asa, to succeed him and rule in Jerusalem because of God's covenant with David. (1 Kings 15:1–8)

Asa 913–873

Asa was the first of the reforming kings in Judah. He purified worship life in Jerusalem by getting rid of the male cult-prostitutes and pagan images, and deposed the queen mother who had made an image of the goddess Asherah. The war with Israel continued during his reign, but he procured Syrian help against Israel using gold and silver taken from the Temple. (1 Kings 15:9–24)

ISRAEL ISRAEL ISRAEL ISRAEL

Jeroboam I 922–901

After the division of the realm into two kingdoms, Jeroboam I used Shechem as his first capital, but later made Penuel and finally Tirzah the seat of the royal residence, 1 Kings 12:25; 14:17; 15:33. Tirzah remained the capital of Israel until about 880 B.C. when Omri made Samaria his capital.

Nadab 901–900

Jeroboam I was followed by his son Nadab, the last of his dynasty. Nadab's brief reign came to an end when Baasha killed him and the entire household of Jeroboam while the Israelites were laying siege to the Philistine city of Gibbethon on Israel's border, thus fulfilling Ahijah's prophecy, 14:10–16. (1 Kings 15:25–32)

Baasha 900–877

The Deuteronomist refers only to the fact that Baasha walked in the ways of Jeroboam, and that he was condemned by Jehu, a prophet. (1 Kings 15:33–16:7)

Elah 877–876

Baasha was succeeded by his son, Elah. Elah and all members of Baasha's household were murdered by Zimri, thus fulfilling the words of the prophet Jehu. (1 Kings 16:8–14)

Zimri 876 (7 days)

Although Zimri ruled for only seven days, the writer condemns him in the same terms as he condemns other kings of Israel. Zimri was succeeded by Omri who marched on the capital, Tirzah, to attack him. Zimri saw the writing on

the wall and committed suicide by setting fire to the royal premises. Israel's soldier then put Omri on the throne. During this period, Tibni, another pretender to the throne, was also eliminated. (1 Kings 16:15–20)

Omri 976–869

Omri ruled for six years at Tirzah and then decided to build a new capital that would reflect more adequately his personal dignity and the future he planned for Israel. The new capital was Samaria. It was planned on a scale similar to Assyrian capitals, complete with a palace to match. Although 1 Kings devotes only a few verses to the reign of Omri (16:25–28), he established a dynasty that lasted through four generations. The Assyrians thought enough of Omri's dynasty to refer to Israel as "the land of Omri" long after his family line ceased to exist. Samaria remained the capital city of the Northern Kingdom until its final destruction by the Assyrians in 721 B.C.

Omri had to cope with threats from the Syrians. To deal with them, he made alliances with Tyre and Judah. To cement relations with the Phoenicians, he married his son Ahab to Jezebel, a princess of Tyre. 1 Kings devotes more attention to the reign of Ahab than it does to the reign of any other northern ruler, largely because of its interest in Elijah and the struggle against Ahab's promotion of Baal worship in Israel. (1 Kings 16:21–28)

Ahab 869–850

During Ahab's reign, the usual rivalry between Israel and Syria continued. Ahab is condemned because he married Jezebel, a Phoenician princess, who seduced him into worshiping false gods. When concluding a pact of friendship with Jehoshaphat of Judah, Ahab arranged for his daughter by Jezebel, Athaliah, to marry Jehoshaphat's son, Jehoram.

The treaty Ahab drew up with the Syrians after defeating them was a lenient one and earned him the displeasure of the prophets, 1 Kings 20. Apparently there was reason for Ahab's course of action. The Assyrians were on the march! Ahab formed a coalition with Syria and other small

Jehoshaphat 874–849

Asa was succeeded by his son Jehoshaphat who had a long reign. Although the Deuteronomist reports little about him, he gives him qualified praise for ridding the land of Temple prostitutes. (1 Kings 22:41–50)

J(eh)oram 849-842

Jehoshaphat was succeeded by his son, Jehoram (the same name as a northern king; he was also known as Joram), who lost control of Edom. The fact that Jehoram married Athaliah, a daughter of Ahab and Jezebel of Israel, indicates the weakness of Judah at this time. The Deuteronomist condemns Jehoram, but states that his punishment was delayed because of God's promise to David.
(2 Kings 8:16–24)

Ahaziah 842

Jehoram's son, Ahaziah, followed his father as king and receives the same strong condemnation given his father. Ahaziah once again joined forces with Jehoram of Israel in another campaign against Syria. Jehoram was wounded in the battle and, while recovering, received a visit from Ahaziah of Judah. (2 Kings 8:25–29)

nations in the area. A confrontation between the Assyrians and this newly formed coalition took place at Qarqar on the Orontes in 853 B.C. Shalmaneser III, the Assyrian king, claimed victory for his forces, but his westward march was temporarily halted by the encounter. The coalition had won breathing space for itself.

War broke out again between Israel and Syria. Ahab's reason for beginning this campaign was that the Israelite town of Ramoth-gilead had not been given to Israel in the treaty drawn up after the previous tussle. Jehoshaphat of Judah added his forces to those of Ahab. Things went badly for the Israel/Judah alliance. Their forces were crushed, Ahab lost his life in the battle, and eventually Jezebel was literally thrown to the dogs and eaten by them, 2 Kings 9:30–37. Fortunately for the southern forces, the Syrians were not able to continue their thrust into Israelite territory. The Assyrians were once again threatening to overrun the Syrian realm. (1 Kings 16:29–22:40)

Ahaziah 850-849

Ahab's son Ahaziah succeeded his father on the throne, but proved to be an ineffective ruler. The Deuteronomist gives him a negative evaluation and adds a story about a conflict between the king and the prophet Elijah. After Ahaziah had an accident and sought an oracle from the god of Ekron, Elijah condemned the king for his lack of faith in the Lord. The king sent his troops to capture Elijah, but each group of soldiers was consumed by fire from the Lord. The message: All efforts to nullify the word of the Lord, spoken by any true prophet, were in vain. (1 Kings 22:51,52; 2 Kings 1:18)

J(eh)oram 849-842

Ahaziah's brother Jehoram followed him as king after only two years. Although Jehoram receives a more positive evaluation than his predecessor, he (like all northern kings) continued in the sin of Jeroboam. (2 Kings 3:1–3)

Jehu 842-815

Second Kings 9:1–3 describes Elisha appointing "one of the sons of the prophets" to anoint Jehu

Athaliah 842–837

Athaliah was the daughter of Ahab of Israel, wife of Jehoram of Judah, and mother of Ahaziah of Judah.

After Jehu killed Ahaziah, Athaliah seized the throne of Judah and ruled for five years. Early in her reign she made strenuous efforts to destroy the Davidic line. However, Joash (or Jehoash), the infant son of Ahaziah, was hidden in the Temple complex by Jehosheba, Ahaziah's sister and the wife of the high priest Jehoiada, 2 Kings 11:2. Judah did not tolerate Athaliah. She was not a member of the Davidic line and she promoted Baal worship. When Joash was seven, he was crowned king in a secret ceremony, Athaliah was murdered, and a Baal temple in Judah was destroyed. (2 Kings 11)

J(eh)oash 837–800

During Joash's early years, Jehoiada acted as regent. Mattan, the priest of the Baal cult, was slain, and pagan images and altars destroyed. Joash is praised for his interest in the Jerusalem Temple, and for devising a method of collecting money that would ensure the ongoing repair of the Temple. Those priests who did not respond when the king took the initiative are criticized. The Deuteronomist says little about Hazael of Syria's incursion into Judah and the assassination of Joash. (2 Kings 12)

as king of Israel. Jehu chose the time of Ahaziah's visit to Jehoram to make his move. He killed Jehoram and Ahaziah, and set himself up as king of Israel. Jonadab, the founder of the Rechabite sect, rode in Jehu's chariot during the murderous spree. Jehu continued his campaign with zeal, destroyed the prophets of Baal in their temple, had Jezebel killed (she was finally eaten by dogs), and inspired the slaughter of the seventy sons of Ahab and all of Ahab's great men, close friends, and priests. Although Jehu killed Jehoram, Ahaziah, and the priests of Baal in a brutal manner, his actions are nonetheless excused in the name of religious zeal. His reign receives a negative evaluation. Although he brought fulfillment to the word of the Lord and removed the Baal cult from Israel, he continued to walk in the ways of Jeroboam. Eventually, Hosea condemned Jehu's action, Hosea 1:14. (1 Kings 21:20–29, 2 Kings 9,10)

It is possible that in killing the kings of both Israel and Judah, Jehu hoped to set himself up as king of a united realm. He did not reckon with Athaliah, the queen mother in Judah, who could be as ruthless as Jehu himself.

Jehoahaz 815–801

Jehu's son, Jehoahaz, followed him on the throne, 2 Kings 10:35. The narrative is typical of those found in Judges. Because Jehoahaz walked in the ways of Jeroboam, the Lord's anger was kindled against him. After Jehoahaz sought the Lord's help, the Lord sent a savior to deliver Israel. Despite the Lord's deliverance, the people continued to walk in the ways of Jeroboam. (2 Kings 13:1–9)

Jehoash 801–786

Jehoahaz's son, Jehoash, succeeded him. In Judah, Amaziah regained control of Edom (2 Kings 14:7) which in turn meant control of its mineral resources. A strange episode followed. Amaziah of Judah challenged Jehoash of Israel to war! Jehoash strove to dissuade Amaziah, but the latter persisted. The consequences for Judah were calamitous. Jerusalem was captured, its Temple plundered, its fortifications destroyed, and hostages were taken to Samaria.

Elisha plays a role in the narrative. He commands King Jehoash to perform certain actions. By these

Amaziah 800-783

Amaziah took over the throne from his father, Joash. He is given qualified approval. Although he pleased the Lord, he did not remove the high places. He honored the Deuteronomic law (Deuteronomy 24:16) by not killing the children of those who had killed his father. The Deuteronomist probably reported Amaziah's challenge to Israel and subsequent defeat because his rash move resulted in the king of Israel plundering the Jerusalem Temple. The Deuteronomist says little about the conspiracy against Amaziah that resulted in his assassination. (2 Kings 14:1–20)

Uzziah (or Azariah) 783-742

Amaziah's son, Uzziah, was made king in his place. He ruled Judah from about 783–742 B.C. Among other things, he rebuilt Elath on the Gulf of Aqabah. Unfortunately for him, he contracted leprosy—possibly because he did not remove the high places. His son Jotham served as his regent (assistant). (2 Kings 15:1–7)

Jotham 742-735

Uzziah was succeeded by his son, Jotham. Jotham ruled with some success for about seven years. He built the upper gate of the Temple, and was attacked by Rezin of Syria and Pekah of Israel in what was the beginning of the Syro-Ephraimitic War. Israel and Syria had joined forces in an attempt to fight the Assyrians, but when Judah refused to join forces with them, they attacked Judah. (2 Kings 15:32–38)

symbolic actions, the king is given power to defend Israel against its enemies. The fact that the king strikes the ground only three times suggests a lack of faith on his part, and thus his victories will be limited. (2 Kings 13:10–25)

Jeroboam II 786-746

Jeroboam II succeeded his father, Jehoash, and ruled from 786–746 B.C. During this period, both Israel and Judah experienced a time of prosperity. Territorially, the two realms almost equaled David's Kingdom. However, the Deuteronomist is concerned above all else that Jeroboam II continued in the sin of Jeroboam I. (2 Kings 14:23–29)

Zechariah 746-745

After Jeroboam II's death in 746 B.C., dynastic turmoil broke out. His son Zechariah ruled only six months and was then murdered by Shallum, thus fulfilling the prophetic word of 2 Kings 10:30. (2 Kings 15:8–12)

Shallum 745

Shallum set himself up as king, but one month later Menahem murdered him. (2 Kings 15:13–16)

Menahem 745-738

Menahem began his reign with atrocities against the expectant mothers of the rebellious city of Tappuah. He soon found himself having to pay tribute to Tiglath-Pileser III of Assyria. The Bible uses his throne name, "Pul." (2 Kings 15:17–22)

Pekahiah 738-737

Menahem was followed by his son Pekahiah who, after a brief reign, was killed by Pekah, possibly because of Pekahiah's willingness to submit to Assyrian overlordship. (2 Kings 15:23–26)

Pekah 737-732

Pekah ruled what was left of Israel, but as an Assyrian vassal, for approximately five years. He was eventually murdered and replaced by Hoshea. (2 Kings 15:27–31, 16:1–20)

Ahaz 735-715

Jotham was succeeded by his son, Ahaz, who inherited not only the throne but the Syro-Ephraimitic War. When Ahaz refused to join Syria and Israel in a coalition against Assyria, Pekah of Israel and Rezin of Damascus joined forces to get rid of Ahaz and replace him with a more cooperative candidate of their own choice. Ahaz is said to have burned his son as an offering—possibly in an effort to arouse divine help. Whatever the reason, Ahaz decided to seek more earthly assistance in the form of Assyrian help—once again at the usual price of the gold and silver in the treasuries of the Temple and royal palace.

Much of the account of Ahaz's reign focuses on a description of the installation of a new altar in the Temple. It was built according to a design that Ahaz had seen in Damascus. The altar *may* have been a symbol of subservience to Assyria. The Deuteronomist views the introduction of the altar as a corruption of the worship in the Temple, and condemns Ahaz for his actions. He is compared to the kings of Israel and accused of introducing the religious practices of Canaan into Judah. (2 Kings 16:1–20)

The Assyrians attacked Israel and Damascus and annexed all but Samaria. The remainder of Israel's territory became the Assyrian provinces of Dor, Megiddo, Karnaim, Hauran, and Gilead, 2 Kings 15:29. Those Israelites considered to be powerful and influential were scattered throughout the Assyrian empire. Judah had managed to buy a respite for a time, but at great cost in money and pride. The nation now became an Assyrian vassal and had to suffer the humiliation of having Assyrian deities placed in the Jerusalem Temple.

Hoshea 732-721

Hoshea tolerated eight years of vassalage to Assyria and then joined ranks with the Egyptians in an attempt to get rid of the Assyrian yoke. At that strategic moment when Shalmaneser V succeeded Tiglath-Pileser on the Assyrian throne, Hoshea declared his intentions by refusing to pay tribute. The new Assyrian king did not view Hoshea's actions kindly. He attacked Israel, threw a siege around Samaria, but died while the campaign was still in progress. His successor, Sargon II, finished the job. Samaria fell in 721 B.C. Many from within Israel were deported. People from around the far-flung Assyrian empire were brought in to replace them. The new arrivals intermarried with the Israelite remnants. The offspring of these unions were known as *Samaritans*.

The kingdom of Israel now came to an end. After their entry into Canaan under Joshua, the Israelites eventually became a united people under one king. In the course of time, the one kingdom broke into two kingdoms, each with its own king. In 721 B.C., the two kingdoms were again reduced to one, this time not by *union* but by *subtraction*. Israel was wiped out; only Judah remained. The Deuteronomist spells out in detail his interpretation of why this catastrophe finally overtook the Northern Kingdom. (2 Kings 17:1–41)

17A After the period of the Judges, Israel was ruled by Saul, David, and Solomon. After Solomon's death, the nation divided into two realms—Israel to the north and Judah to the south. The Northern Kingdom of Israel was ruled by a succession of 19 kings from nine dynasties—until its destruction by Assyria in 721 B.C. The Southern Kingdom of Judah was ruled by David's descendants (with one exception: Queen Athaliah) until it was destroyed by the Babylonians in 587 B.C.

17B Because of the fertility of the soil within the borders of Israel, its citizens were able to produce greater quantities of meat, grain, and fruit products than could those living in less-fertile Judah to the south. Furthermore, because Israel shared borders with Phoenicia, the northerners were able to partner with the Phoenicians (a sea-faring people) to market their goods around the Mediterranean.

Neither Israel nor Judah could live in isolation from surrounding nations. To the north and south were Assyria, Babylon, and Egypt—each with its own dream of empire. Later came the Persians, Greeks, and Romans. Other lesser powers which also made life difficult for God's people were Syria, Philistia, Moab, and Edom.

17C The narrative that unfolds in 1 and 2 Kings reflects the spirit of Deuteronomy:

- God blesses those who obey Him, and punishes those who do not.
- Worship and sacrifice must be offered to God in one place—Jerusalem.

17D When evaluating the worth of all kings of Israel and Judah, the writer:

- denigrates all northern kings; they walked in the ways of Jeroboam, the first king of Israel, and prevented their people from worshiping Israel's one God in Jerusalem.
- approves only those southern kings who walked in the ways of David, worshiped one God in Jerusalem, and encouraged their subjects to do the same.

17E Nine dynasties (families of kings) ruled in the Northern Kingdom. In seven cases, the takeover of a reigning dynasty by another was achieved by assassination. One northern king committed suicide after ruling for only seven days.

Although five assassinations took place in the Southern Kingdom of Judah, there was no change in dynasty. The ruler who was put to death was succeeded by his son—and all were descendants of David. The only exception was Athaliah, who—after her husband died and her son was killed—grabbed the throne of Judah. However, she was eventually executed and replaced by her grandson, Joash—a legitimate descendant of David.

17F 1 and 2 Kings contain numerous narratives that describe the work of the prophet Elijah, and his successor Elisha.

17G The kings of Israel and Judah sometimes cooperated with each other, sometimes fought each other, and sometimes entangled themselves in the affairs of surrounding nations. Eventually in 721 B.C., the Assyrians brought the history of the Northern Kingdom to an end, scattered many of its citizens around their vast empire, and intermarried those left behind with people they brought in from nearby nations.

Although Judah continued as a political entity, it came under the control of the Assyrians, then the Egyptians (609–605 B.C.), and finally the Babylonians, 605–539 B.C.

CROSS WAYS

2 SECTION

UNITS 11–20

From the Conquest to the Babylonian Exile

UNIT 18

Judah's Last Years

The History of Judah from 721 B.C. to 560 B.C.

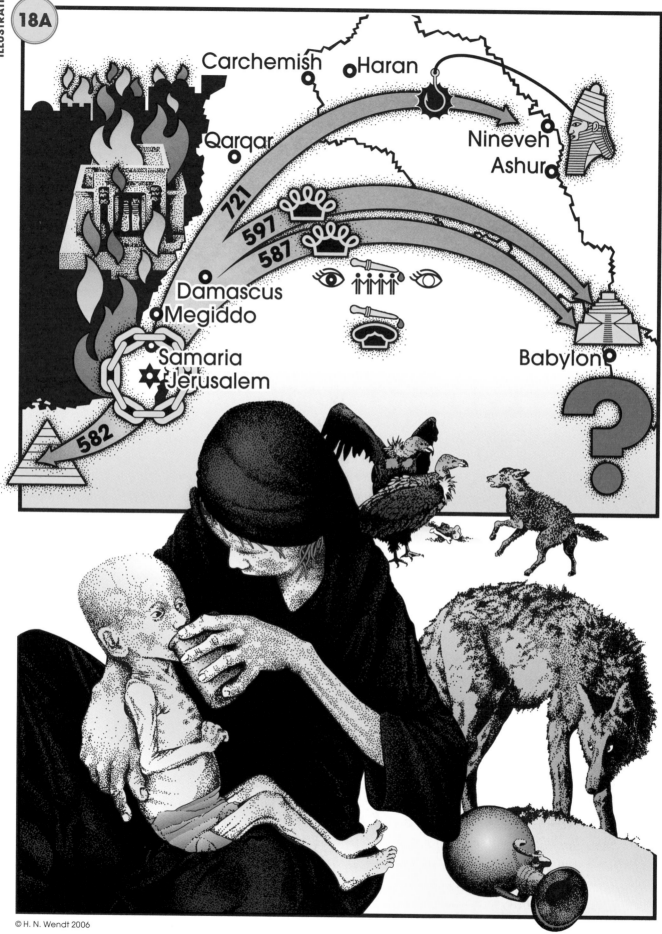

Carchemish
Haran
Qarqar
Nineveh
Ashur
721
597
587
Damascus
Megiddo
Samaria
Jerusalem
Babylon
582

2 Kings 18–25

ILLUSTRATION 18A summarizes events associated with the last days of Israel and later, Judah.

1 *Qarqar:* An alliance of nations (including Israel, Judah, and Syria) fought with Assyrian forces at Qarqar in 853 B.C. and managed to delay further advances by the Assyrians into their regions. *Damascus* was (and still is) the capital of Syria.

2 *Arrow to Nineveh and Ashur, Assyrian king:* The Assyrians devastated the Northern Kingdom of Israel and its capital, *Samaria*, in *721* B.C., and took many of its citizens into exile. To ensure that those being led into exile would cause no problems along the way, the Assyrians ran a *fishhook* through their nose and tied them nose-to-nose.

The Assyrians resettled many people from around their vast empire into the former Northern Kingdom, and had them intermarry with the remaining Israelites. Those born of these mixed marriages were known as the *Samaritans*. They accepted the Pentateuch as their sacred writings and worshiped the God of the patriarchs and the Exodus on Mt. Gerizim.

3 *Carchemish:* Pharaoh Thutmoses III (ca. 1490–1436 B.C.) claimed Carchemish for Egypt. It served as an Egyptian fortress outpost to prevent Mesopotamian military campaigns into the land of the Nile. It eventually served as a Hittite fortress, but became independent in 1110 B.C. In 717 B.C., it came under Assyrian control. In 609 B.C., Pharaoh Neco of Egypt traveled north via *Megiddo* (where he killed Josiah of Judah, 2 Kings 23:29,30) to recapture Carchemish and establish it as a base for harassing the Babylonians. The Egyptians then controlled Judah until 605 B.C., when the Babylonians captured Judah and made it part of their empire.

4 *Arrows pointing to Babylon, ziggurat:* In *597* B.C., the Babylonians put down a revolt in Judah and took King Jehoiachin (*crown*) and many of Judah's leading citizens into exile (*circle of chains around Jerusalem*) in Babylon, 2 Kings 24:10–17. The Babylonians crushed a second revolt in *587* B.C., blinded King Zedekiah (*eyes*) after killing his sons (*dagger above four figures*), killed many political and religious leaders (*dagger above priest's hat*), and took a second group of people, including King Zedekiah (*crown*), into exile, 2 Kings 25:1–21.

5 *Temple, Jerusalem skyline, flames* (*top left*): The Babylonians under Nebuchadnezzar plundered and destroyed Jerusalem and its Temple in *587* B.C.

6 *Malnourished mother and child:* Deuteronomy had warned that neglect of the covenant would cause devastating hardships or curses, Deuteronomy 28:20–24,47–51. See also Jeremiah 14:15,16; 18:21; 29:17,18.

7 *Dogs and birds:* Animals and birds would consume the bodies of the people who had forgotten God's covenant mercy and will, Deuteronomy 28:26; Jeremiah 16:4.

8 *Pyramid; arrow to Egypt:* After destroying Jerusalem in 587 B.C., the Babylonians appointed Gedaliah as governor of Judah. When Ishmael (a descendant of David), encouraged by Baalis, king of the Ammonites, killed Gedaliah in *582* B.C., many of those remaining in Judah fled to Egypt, and demanded that Jeremiah and his scribe, Baruch, go with them, Jeremiah 40:7–43:7; 2 Kings 25:22–26.

9 When Jehoiachin died in Babylon some time after 560 B.C. (2 Kings 25:27–30), it appeared that the Davidic dynasty had come to an end. In 538 B.C., some of the exiles in Babylon began to return to Judah. They were known as *Jews* and from them came *Judaism*. They insisted that sacrifices must be offered to God only in the Jerusalem Temple.

The Northern Kingdom was destroyed by the Assyrians in 721 B.C. The Babylonians invaded Judah and carried its people into exile in 597 and 587 B.C. What follows is a summary of events and the kingships that ruled Judah between these two catastrophes.

Ahaz (2 Kings 16:1–20)

1 Ahaz succeeded his father Jotham on the throne of Judah and ruled from 735–715 B.C. When threatened by the coalition forces of Syria and Israel, Ahaz called on Tiglath-pileser of Assyria for help. Ahaz depleted the treasuries of both his palace and the Jerusalem Temple to purchase this help—which most likely would have come without his request (the Assyrians would have been supportive of any realm that refused to revolt against them). Although Judah survived the attempt to force it to join in the rebellion against Assyria, Judah now found itself a vassal of that very country which had come to its aid. Judah was in a pitiful state. To complicate matters, the Assyrian frontier was now only a few miles north of Jerusalem.

2 The Assyrian king summoned Ahaz to Damascus to swear allegiance to him. As a result of his visit, Ahaz carried out a number of changes within the Jerusalem Temple. He moved the main altar of the Temple to one side and replaced it with an Assyrian altar. This may have been a way of acknowledging Assyrian overlordship in a manner typical of the times. It is also possible that Ahaz was paying genuine respect to a foreign religion. Some of his previous religious actions had been pagan; he "sacrificed and made offerings on the high places, on the hills, and under every green tree" (2 Kings 16:4)—a comment indicating that Ahaz dabbled in the fertility cults. He also burned his son as a sacrifice (2 Kings 16:3), perhaps at the time when the Israel-Syria alliance was laying siege to Jerusalem. Finally, Ahaz dismantled some of the bronze equipment in the Temple court, most likely to make the required tribute payments to Assyria. Things were at a low ebb. Temple equipment was being melted down to buy off the Assyrians.

Hezekiah (2 Kings 18:1–20:21)

1 Ahaz was succeeded by his son, Hezekiah, who ruled from 715–687 B.C. A problem involving chronology occurs in the text; 18:9–12 suggests that the destruction of Israel took place in the fourth year of Hezekiah's reign. This is unlikely if Hezekiah came to the throne in 715 B.C., six years after the Assyrian destruction of Israel in 721 B.C.

2 Hezekiah's policies were different from those of Ahaz. To begin with, Hezekiah took steps to bring about important religious reforms. He made efforts to rid Judah of pagan cult objects and practices and to centralize all worship in Jerusalem, 2 Kings 18:1–6,22.

3 Ahaz chose to submit to the Assyrian yoke; Hezekiah chose to throw it off, 18:7. Encouragement for this course of action came also from beyond Judah's borders, for some of Hezekiah's neighbors (who were also vassals of Assyria) also longed for independence. The time seemed ripe for revolt. Sargon of Assyria was trying to cope with problems that demanded the consolidation of Assyrian power *to the north*. To complicate matters for the Assyrian ruler, Marduk-apal-iddina (referred to as Merodach-baladan in 2 Kings 20:12) had driven the Assyrians from Babylonia and declared his independence. Sargon devoted twelve years to dealing with this latter problem. Furthermore, the Egyptians *to the south* fanned the flames of Judah's nationalism, urged it to revolt, and promised aid. Independence from Assyria seemed to be a possibility.

4 A rebellion against Assyria broke out in the Philistine city of Ashdod in 711 B.C., and both Assyrian records and Isaiah 20 indicate that efforts were made to have Judah join in the uprising. Fortunately for Judah, Hezekiah took no part in the revolt. It took the Assyrians very little time to squash the opposition. Years before, Isaiah had urged Ahaz not to make overtures to the Assyrians when threatened by the Syro-Israel coalition. Now he declared himself against any attempt to rebel against them, possibly because he was well aware of the futility of such a move. The prophet walked through the streets of Jerusalem naked and barefoot to paint a living picture of the end result of any attempt to throw off the Assyrian yoke, Isaiah 20. Isaiah also insisted on this occasion, as on others, that any promise of help from the Egyptians should be taken with a grain of salt. Security and strength were not to be found in military might, but in a quiet trust in God, Isaiah 7:3–9; 28:14–22; 30:1–17.

5. Sargon of Assyria died in 705 B.C. and was succeeded by his son Sennacherib. Once again, the time seemed ripe for Judah to revolt. A second uprising had taken place in Babylonia under Marduk-apal-iddina and was keeping Sennacherib occupied. Out to the west a coalition was formed, consisting of a number of Syrian and Palestinian states, with backing from the Egyptians. According to 2 Kings 20:12–19, Marduk-apal-iddina of Babylon sent envoys to Hezekiah to encourage him to join them. 2 Chronicles 32:3–5 speaks of Hezekiah taking measures to improve Jerusalem's defenses and the nation's military strength. Most likely Hezekiah's famous conduit (*tunnel*) was dug about this time to ensure Jerusalem's water supply during a time of siege, 2 Kings 20:20.

6. The Assyrians lost little time in dealing with the uprising and swept through the entire region to wreak vengeance. Their forces subdued Phoenicia and captured the coastal cities of Bethdagon, Joppa, Benai-barka, Azuru, Ekron, Eltekeh, and Timnath. An Egyptian army was devastated at Eltekeh. Forty-six of Judah's fortified cities were razed; Jerusalem was not. Sennacherib made Lachish his headquarters while he laid siege to Jerusalem, from which he extracted a heavy tribute. However, the Assyrians packed up and left without forcing Jerusalem to surrender, 2 Kings 18:13–19:37; Isaiah 36–37. Hints of trouble at home possibly contributed to the Assyrian departure, Isaiah 37:7. 2 Kings 19:35 attributes the Assyrian withdrawal to a plague sent by God.

7. Isaiah's pronouncements during this uprising were significant. He had previously insisted that any attempt to revolt from Assyria was a covenant with death; God was using Assyria as His instrument of judgment on sinful Judah. However, in 701 B.C. Isaiah assured a terrified Hezekiah that Jerusalem would not fall to the Assyrians; God would defend it for His own sake and for the sake of His servant David, 2 Kings 19:1–4; Isaiah 37:21–35.

8. Although Isaiah predicted that the Assyrian king would return to his land and be killed (2 Kings 19:6,7), Sennacherib was not killed until 681 B.C., twenty years after withdrawing his forces from Jerusalem. The reality was that Judah escaped with its life, but with little more. Although Jerusalem was not ravaged, the surrounding countryside was. Hezekiah remained a vassal of Assyria throughout the remainder of his reign.

9. The Deuteronomist outlines the events of Hezekiah's reign to conform to the theological perspective set out in 2 Kings 17:34–39. He stresses that Hezekiah feared and worshiped the Lord alone, and rid the Temple of pagan elements. God showed His power over Assyria and His approval of Hezekiah's reform by delivering Jerusalem. The Deuteronomist ignores the fact that Hezekiah remained a vassal of Assyria.

10. Isaiah features prominently in the final two stories. First, he heals the king, showing that God blessed Hezekiah for his faithfulness, 20:1–11. Second, Isaiah's reaction to Hezekiah's meeting with the king of Babylon shows that doom was sure to overtake Jerusalem, 20:12–19.

Manasseh (2 Kings 21:1–18)

1. It was still an Assyrian world. Although Sennacherib was assassinated in 681 B.C., his son Esarhaddon (681–669 B.C.) and his successor Ashurbanipal (669–633 B.C.) pushed Assyrian frontiers further afield until their empire became larger than any the world had previously known. They achieved victory wherever they went. Babylonia was subdued, and in 671 B.C. an invasion was launched against Egypt. In 663 B.C. Thebes was taken and destroyed. The conquest of Egypt meant that the only nation capable of offering any help in revolts against Assyria was gone.

2 During much of this period of Assyrian ascendancy, Manasseh sat on the throne of Judah. He ruled 687–642 B.C. While he ruled, Judah sank into the depths of false worship. No doubt political necessity contributed to this state of affairs. During Manasseh's time, Assyrian deities were worshiped, divination and magic practiced, altars to the heavenly bodies and astral deities set up in the Jerusalem Temple, the rite of ordeal by fire permitted, and the fertility cults restored, 2 Kings 21:1–9. Manasseh is dismissed as the worst king ever to sit on the throne of Judah. His sin could never be forgiven, and this was enough to explain why the nation eventually came to ruin, 2 Kings 21:10–15. Not only did he tolerate and encourage false worship of every kind, but he also persecuted those wishing to remain faithful to the God of their fathers, 2 Kings 21:16. The evil that Manasseh did outweighed the good Josiah (his grandson) did, with the result that, despite Josiah's reform measures, Judah still had to go into exile in Babylon, 2 Kings 23:25–27.

3 A different account occurs in 2 Chronicles 33:1–20; see 33:10–13, where it is said that Manasseh was taken to Babylon, that he repented while there, and was restored to the throne in Jerusalem. Whatever repentance Manasseh felt must have been temporary, for the abuses and apostasy he introduced into Judah and the Temple remained in place until Josiah removed them, 2 Kings 23:4–14.

Amon (2 Kings 21:19–26)

Amon's two-year reign (642–640 B.C.) was one that perpetuated the policies and actions of his father Manasseh. After only two years on the throne, he was killed in a palace conspiracy—possibly by people dissatisfied with his continuing submission to Assyria. Amon was replaced by his son, Josiah.

Josiah (2 Kings 22:1–23:30)

1 Josiah is the favorite of those who wrote 1 and 2 Kings (2 Kings 23:25; but see also 2 Kings 18:5). He was one of Judah's most important rulers. Josiah was placed on the throne at the tender age of eight and ruled for 31 years, 640–609 B.C.

2 Once again the affairs of Judah were intertwined with the fortunes of Assyria. Although Assyria was still a force to be reckoned with, Assyria's last effective ruler was Ashurbanipal, 669–630 B.C. After the latter's death, Josiah was in a position to begin measures to achieve religious reform and political independence.

3 Most likely, Josiah had limited authority, with Assyrian permission, over what formerly had been the Northern Kingdom. As Assyrian power and influence waned, Josiah claimed control over both realms, possibly with a view to reestablishing a United Kingdom under a single Davidic monarchy. After Ashurbanipal died, Josiah removed the gods of his Assyrian overlord from the Jerusalem Temple ("the vessels made for all the host of heaven," 23:4; the altars of Ahaz and Manasseh, 23:12)—an action that declared independence from Assyrian control. In addition, he rid the Jerusalem Temple of the paraphernalia and practices that had been there since the time of Manasseh. His measures for reform were not confined to Jerusalem and its precincts, but were undertaken throughout Judah and Israel as well.

4 The account in 2 Chronicles 34,35 suggests that the reform took place *before* a certain book of the law was discovered in the Temple. The account in 2 Kings suggests that it took place *after* the discovery of the book in question, and that *the contents of the book inspired the reform movement*. Most likely the book was Deuteronomy, or at least a version of Deuteronomy 12–26. Unit 19 will probe this issue a little further.

5 Assyria was now breathing its last. Babylonian forces captured **Ashur** in 614 B.C. and **Nineveh** in 612 B.C. The Assyrian forces were pushed back to the vicinity of **Haran**. The impending collapse of Assyria alarmed Pharaoh Neco of Egypt, who saw Babylon's rise as a threat to the prevailing balance of power. In 609 B.C. Neco led his army northwards to help the ailing Assyria. Josiah intervened—and joined in battle against the Egyptian forces at **Megiddo**. Although it is possible that he objected to the Egyptians trespassing in his realm, it is more likely that he wanted to stop the Egyptians from giving support to Judah's traditional enemy. Josiah lost his life in the encounter, and Judah became a vassal of Egypt, 2 Kings 23:29,30.

Jehoahaz (2 Kings 23:31–34)

The people of Judah placed Josiah's son, Shallum, on the throne after his father's death in 609 B.C. His throne name was Jehoahaz. After he had ruled for three months, Pharaoh Neco sent him into exile in Egypt and replaced him with another son of Josiah, Eliakim, whose throne name was Jehoiakim.

Jehoiakim (2 Kings 23:35–24:7)

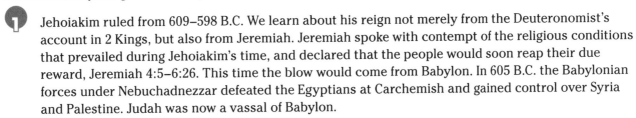

Jehoiakim ruled from 609–598 B.C. We learn about his reign not merely from the Deuteronomist's account in 2 Kings, but also from Jeremiah. Jeremiah spoke with contempt of the religious conditions that prevailed during Jehoiakim's time, and declared that the people would soon reap their due reward, Jeremiah 4:5–6:26. This time the blow would come from Babylon. In 605 B.C. the Babylonian forces under Nebuchadnezzar defeated the Egyptians at Carchemish and gained control over Syria and Palestine. Judah was now a vassal of Babylon.

In 605 B.C. Nabopolassar, king of Babylon, died, and Nebuchadnezzar took his place. In 601 B.C. the Egyptians managed to inflict a defeat on the Babylonians. Possibly this moved Jehoiakim to try to gain freedom for Judah by rebelling against Babylon. The Babylonians dealt with the uprising by invading Judah. Fortunately for Jehoiakim, he died shortly before their forces captured Jerusalem. His son Jehoiachin succeeded him.

Jehoiachin (2 Kings 24:8–17)

Jehoiachin's rule was a brief one. The Babylonians set siege to Jerusalem in 598 B.C., and in March of 597 the city capitulated. Nebuchadnezzar exacted a heavy tribute, sent the king and many others into exile in Babylon, and set up a king of his own choice in Jehoiachin's place.

Zedekiah (2 Kings 24:18–25:7)

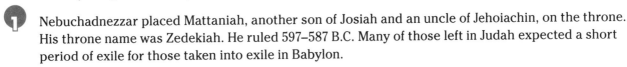

Nebuchadnezzar placed Mattaniah, another son of Josiah and an uncle of Jehoiachin, on the throne. His throne name was Zedekiah. He ruled 597–587 B.C. Many of those left in Judah expected a short period of exile for those taken into exile in Babylon.

Zedekiah accepted Jeremiah's counsel and submitted to the Babylonian yoke. However, pro-Egyptian elements in his court forced a rebellion in 589 B.C. Once again, the Babylonian forces set out for Judah and set siege to Jerusalem. In 587 B.C., the city fell. Zedekiah was captured and brought before Nebuchadnezzar at Riblah on the Orontes. He was forced to watch while his sons were killed one by one. It would be the last thing he would ever see. His eyes were then put out, and he was taken in chains to Babylon. A second deportation took place later that year.

A final note in 2 Kings 25:27–30 refers to the fact that Jehoiachin, a descendant of David, was still alive in Babylon in 560 B.C. The hope was that the nation might soon return to Judah and that the Davidic dynasty would be restored through the person of Jehoiachin.

18C

1. **Do we need a prince/king?**
   (1 Samuel 8–12)
   ☐ Yes
   ☐ No

2. **Whose dynasty?**
   (1 Sam. 13 – 2 Sam. 2, 6, 7, 9, 21)
   ☐ Saul's (Benjamin)
   ☐ David's (Judah)

3. **The extent of David's kingdom?** (2 Samuel 2, 5, 8, 10)

4. **Who will succeed David?**
   (2 Samuel 11–1 Kings 2)
   ☐ Amnon
   ☐ Absalom
   ☐ Adonijah
   ☐ Solomon

5. **What determines the worth of a king?** (Kings & Chronicles)
   ☐ Is he a descendant of David?
   ☐ Does he worship one God in one place?

6. **The fate of the Davidic dynasty beyond 587** (2 Kings 25:27–30)
   ☐ To end?
   ☐ To continue?

7. **What will the messianic age/king be like?**

Questions Raised by the History of Kings 18C

1. Do we need a prince/king?

The debate as to whether or not Israel should have kings is reported in 1 Samuel 8–12. See Unit 14.

2. Whose dynasty?

Although Samuel appointed Saul as Israel's first king, Saul earned the disfavor of the prophetic community (represented by Samuel, 1 Samuel 13) and the priestly community (1 Samuel 22:6–23). Samuel appointed David as Saul's successor even while Saul was still alive, 1 Samuel 16.

In 2 Samuel 2:1–4, David is made king of Judah. In 2 Samuel 6, Saul's daughter (and David's wife), Michal, is excluded from David's bedroom after accusing her husband of indecent exposure; see vv. 16,20,23. In 2 Samuel 7:1–17, David is promised a dynasty, a line of kings. In 2 Samuel 9, David takes Jonathan's son into his palace, possibly to ensure that he makes no attempt to reestablish Saul's dynasty. In 2 Samuel 21, David permits the Gibeonites to kill two of Saul's sons (and David's brothers-in-law) and five of Saul's grandsons (David's nephews).

3. The extent of David's kingdom?

After Saul's death (1 Samuel 31), David gains control of Judah (1 Samuel 2:2–4), and Israel (2 Samuel 5:1–5), and captures and annexes a number of surrounding nations (2 Samuel 8,10).

4. Who will succeed David?

After David commits adultery with Bathsheba, Nathan tells him that many family problems will overtake him, 2 Samuel 11,12. His oldest son, *Amnon*, rapes his half-sister Tamar, and two years later is killed by her full brother, *Absalom*, 2 Samuel 13. After Absalom revolts against David in hope of gaining the throne, he is killed by David's general, Joab, 2 Samuel 15–18. Although *Adonijah* hopes to succeed David when the latter is found to be impotent (1 Kings 1:1–10), he is upstaged by Nathan and Bathsheba, who perpetrate an intrigue that places *Solomon* on the throne, 1 Kings 1:11–48.

5. What determines the worth of a king?

In determining the worth of a king, the writers of Kings and Chronicles ask two questions:

- Is he a descendant of David?
- Does he worship *one God in one place*—the Jerusalem Temple?

6. The fate of the Davidic dynasty beyond 587 B.C?

The Babylonians put down a revolt in Judah in 597 B.C., and in 587 B.C. put down a second revolt and destroyed Judah and Jerusalem. In 597 B.C. the Babylonians took Jehoiachin, Judah's king, into exile. According to 2 Kings 25:27–30, Jehoiachin was still alive in 560 B.C. The exiles in Babylon therefore saw cause for hope. Perhaps they would return to Judah, and (the still alive) Jehoiachin would assume the throne once again and restore the Davidic dynasty. However, Jehoiachin died in Babylon.

7. What will the messianic age/king be like?

The postexilic community lived under foreign domination for hundreds of years. They looked forward to the time when God would give them political freedom and reestablish the Davidic dynasty. They believed that when these two dreams were fulfilled, they would experience the messianic age. Various views were held regarding what the messianic kingdom and king would be like. Some thought it would be a time when all in Israel would sit under their own *vine and fig tree* (Micah 4:4), and God would destroy all of Israel's enemies, Micah 4:9–13, 5:7–9 (*sword*). However, Jesus of Nazareth proved a shock and a disappointment to them!

18A Although the Northern Kingdom was destroyed by the Assyrians in 721 B.C. and many of its citizens taken into exile, the Southern Kingdom continued. Judah became a vassal of Assyria in 735 B.C., and remained under Assyrian domination until 609 B.C.

As the seventh century B.C. drew to a close, Assyria began to crumble. In 609 B.C., Egypt set out to prop up a dying Assyria so that it might serve as a buffer against a rising Babylonia. Josiah tried to stop the Egyptian forces marching through his realm on their way to Assyria—but lost the battle and his life at Megiddo. Judah now came under Egyptian control. When Babylonian forces conquered the Egyptians in 605 B.C., Judah came under Babylonian control.

Eventually Jehoiakim of Judah (609–597 B.C.) joined a coalition seeking independence from Babylon. Nebuchadnezzar acted swiftly. He set siege to Jerusalem, and, in 597 B.C., the city capitulated. Jehoiakim—who died before the fall of Jerusalem in 597 B.C.—was succeeded by his son, Jehoiachin, who was taken into exile in Babylon after only three months on the throne. When a brother and successor of Jehoiakim, Zedekiah, sought to rid Judah of Babylonian control a few years later, Nebuchadnezzar again set siege to Jerusalem. The city was destroyed in 587 B.C. Deportations to Babylon took place after both catastrophes. Some of those left in Judah eventually fled to Egypt—the land from which their ancestors had been rescued long before.

18B The writer of Kings continued to use as his yardstick for evaluating the worth of Judean kings their attitude toward the worship of the one God in the Jerusalem Temple. Of the nine kings that ruled after the destruction of Israel, only Hezekiah and Josiah receive commendation. Both made strenuous efforts to rid the Temple of the paraphernalia of the pagan cults. Likewise, both attempted to gain independence from Assyria and regain control over what was left of the former Northern Kingdom.

18C The narrative in 1 Samuel–2 Kings is complex.

- The Promised Land was first ruled by prophets such as Eli, and prophets-judges such as Samuel.

- It was then ruled by Saul (from Benjamin), and David and Solomon (from Judah).

- David established a realm of considerable size.

- A brutal struggle for the throne took place among David's sons—with Solomon emerging as the winner.

- For any king, whether from Israel or Judah, to be approved, he had to be a descendant of David, and practice and promote the worship of *one God in one place*, Jerusalem.

- After the Babylonians destroyed Judah and Jerusalem in 587 B.C. and took two of its kings (Jehoiachin in 597 and Zedekiah in 587) into exile, the exiles asked, "What is our future to be? Will the Davidic dynasty ever be restored?"

- After the exiles began to return to Judah in 538 B.C., they remained under the control of a succession of foreign powers: Persians, Greeks, Ptolemies, Seleucids, and Romans. Although they longed for the coming of a messianic king, they thought of that king as a political figure who would restore David's realm and rule.

CROSS WAYS®

2 SECTION

UNITS 11–20

From the Conquest to the Babylonian Exile

UNIT 19

Josiah's Reform

The Centralization of Worship in Jerusalem in 621 B.C.

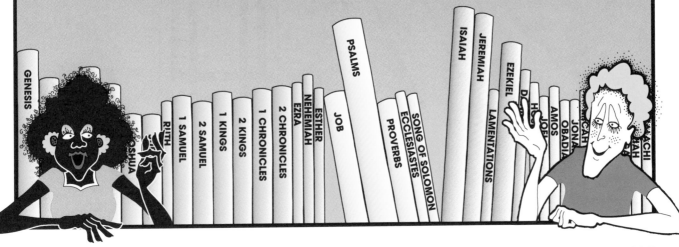

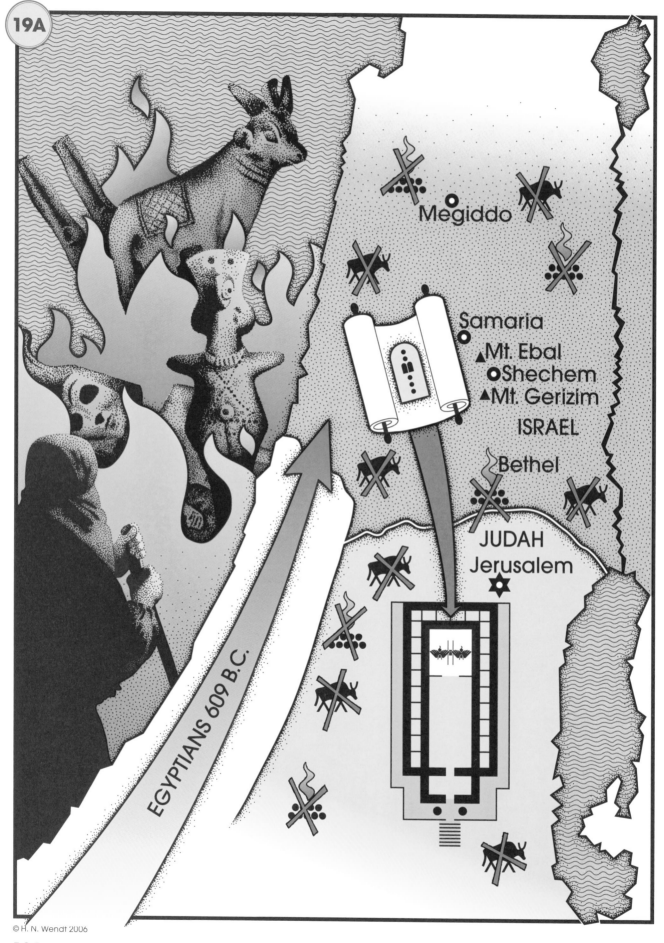

Megiddo

Samaria
▲Mt. Ebal
○Shechem
▲Mt. Gerizim

ISRAEL

Bethel

JUDAH
Jerusalem

EGYPTIANS 609 B.C.

© H. N. Wendt 2006

106

ILLUSTRATION 19A depicts the events outlined in 2 Kings 22,23: the centralization of worship and the sacrificial system in the Jerusalem Temple in 621 B.C. (All references below are from 2 Kings, unless otherwise indicated.)

1 In 621 B.C., Josiah, king of Judah, arranged to have the ***Jerusalem Temple*** repaired, 2 Kings 22:3. While these repairs were in progress, Josiah sent Shaphan, one of his officials, to the High Priest, Hilkiah, to pay the carpenters, builders, and stone masons involved in the project, 22:3–7.

2 During Shaphan's meeting with the High Priest, Hilkiah told him that he had found "the book of the law" (***scroll, with symbol for covenant superimposed***) in the Temple and gave it to Shaphan. Shaphan told King Josiah about the discovery, and read the book to him, 22:8–10. The book's contents greatly disturbed Josiah, who then set up a delegation to provide him with an interpretation of the book's message, 22:14–20.

3 The delegation sought the help of Huldah, a prophetess, to obtain the requested interpretation. (Although Jeremiah was carrying out his ministry at this time, his advice was not sought.) Huldah told the members of the delegation that because the people were worshiping false gods, disaster was about to overtake the nation. Jerusalem would soon become "a desolation and a curse," 22:14–20. But because Josiah had been penitent and faithful, he would be spared—and "gathered to his grave in peace," v. 20.

4 Josiah then led a covenant ceremony in which he pledged "to follow the Lord, keeping his commandments, his decrees, and his statutes, with all his heart and all his soul, to perform the words of this covenant that were written in this book." All present joined in the ritual, 23:1–3. The events which followed were of great importance:

- Josiah removed from the Temple objects used in Baal worship and Assyrian astral worship, burned them (***calf, idol, image, royal worker***, *top left*), and dumped their ashes at ***Bethel***, 23:4,5. The royal shrine of the former Northern Kingdom had been located at Bethel; see Amos 7:10–12. Southern priests hated Bethel! They insisted that God's people should worship God in only one place—***Jerusalem***.

- Josiah closed all shrines in Judah, leaving the Jerusalem Temple as the only legitimate place for offering sacrifice. Some of the outlying shrines were probably shrines in which the God of Israel was worshiped—even though their priests were referred to as "idolatrous" because even an *orthodox* shrine located outside of Jerusalem was now viewed as *idolatrous*, 23:5. Some outlying shrines were pagan; the people worshiped the Baals and Assyrian astral deities in them, 23:5b. (*Orthodox shrines are depicted by* ***altars of stones***. *Pagan shrines are depicted by a* ***bull***. ***All are shown crossed out*** *to signify that they are all now considered invalid.*) It is important to note that Josiah invited the priests who served at the "idolatrous" shrines (23:5a) to join the staff of the Jerusalem Temple, 23:9. *He would not have done this had they been pagan.* However, these priests chose to remain living where they were, 23:9.

- Josiah then cleansed Jerusalem and the Temple by getting rid of all signs of Baal worship, male temple prostitutes, women who wove hangings for goddesses, child sacrifice, horses and chariots dedicated to the sun, altars linked to Ahaz and Manasseh, the idolatrous shrines that Solomon had built some 300 years earlier, and "mediums, wizards, teraphim, idols, and other abominations," 23:6–14,24.

- Next, Josiah smashed *all shrines in what had been the Northern Kingdom*, burned human bones on their altars to defile them, and killed all the priests who served in them (they were not Levites, 1 Kings 12:31), 23:15–20. Specific mention is made of the shrine at Bethel—that remnant of "Jeroboam's sin," 1 Kings 12:29,30. Even though the God of Israel was worshiped at some northern shrines, the issue related to *centralization, geographical validity, control, and the growing power of the Jerusalem priests*.

- Finally, Josiah commanded that a Passover celebration be held in Jerusalem—now the only valid place for offering sacrifice, 23:21–23.

5 Josiah was killed in ***609 B.C.*** at ***Megiddo*** while trying to prevent the ***Egyptians from marching north*** to prop up a dying Assyria as a buffer against an expanding Babylonian empire, 23:28–30.

1 After the death of Ashurbanipal of Assyria, conditions in the Ancient Near East favored the rebirth of Judean nationalism. Although Assyria was losing its grip on the Fertile Crescent, its collapse did not take place overnight. About the time of Josiah's reform, the prophets Jeremiah and Zephaniah were predicting that the existing world order was about to crumble.

2 To the east, Nabopolassar of Babylonia (625–605 B.C.) managed to rid his realm of Assyrian control. Encouraged by this, Josiah removed all Assyrian elements from the worship life of Judah. He was supported in this by "the people of the land" (see 11:14,19 and 21:23,24) who earlier had opposed Manasseh's submission to the Assyrian yoke and longed for national independence.

3 In cleansing the Temple, Josiah removed objects associated with Assyrian worship of the heavenly bodies (23:4,5) and the altars that Ahaz and Manasseh had placed in its precincts, 23:12. In removing these, Josiah was doing more than carrying out a religious reform; he was declaring that he would no longer submit to Assyria, whose authority and control over Judah these objects symbolized! Assyrian rule was now a thing of the past.

4 Other motivating factors in Josiah's reform were:

- Judah's religious beliefs must never be blended with those of surrounding nations. The faith of the nation's "founding fathers" (*and no other!*) must prevail!
- The nation's relationship with God needed to be restored and revitalized to spare it from the fate that had overtaken the Northern Kingdom and from the curses the law book said would fall on God's people if they ignored God's commandments, Deuteronomy 28:15–68.

JOSIAH'S PASSOVER CELEBRATION

1 After the reform measures described above, Josiah commanded the people to hold a Passover observance in Jerusalem, 23:21–23. The account of the first Passover is given in Exodus 12. Instructions concerning its observance are given in Numbers 9 and Deuteronomy 16. Joshua 5:10–12 states that Israel observed a Passover at Gilgal soon after crossing the Jordan. The only other *preexilic* references to a Passover being observed took place during the reign of Hezekiah, 2 Chronicles 30. A *postexilic* observance is mentioned in Ezra 6:19,20.

2 How are we to interpret 2 Kings 23:21–23, especially the words "no *such* Passover"? Had Israel not been observing Passover? The text does not say that. The key thought is contained in the words, "as prescribed in this book of the covenant," 23:21. If the book found in the Temple was Deuteronomy (see 19C), the significant factor in relation to Josiah's reform was that the Passover was being observed by the whole nation in *one place*—something demanded by many passages in Deuteronomy (e.g., 12:5,11,14,18,21,26), even though those passages never specify the name of that *one place*.

3 At the time of Joshua, the nation was present at *one place*, in *Gilgal*, when it observed the Passover, Joshua 5:10–12. At the time of Josiah, the nation again observed the Passover in *one place*, in *Jerusalem*; see 23:22. After Josiah destroyed all shrines in Judah and the former Northern Kingdom, only one legitimate shrine remained in the land: *the Jerusalem Temple*. The worship life of the nation was now centralized in one place!

4 Although Josiah ruled for 31 years (from 640 until 609 B.C. when he was killed by the Egyptians), the writer of Kings was content to report only what he did in relation to the Jerusalem Temple in 621 B.C. A major concern in *Deuteronomy through 2 Kings* is that God's people should worship *one God in one place*. **That one place was now the Jerusalem Temple.**

THE IDENTITY OF THE LAW BOOK

1 The events outlined in 2 Kings 22 and 23 offer clues about the identity of the law book discovered in the Temple. It must have been a book that strongly condemned the paganism (such as that which had seeped into Judah's life during the reign of Manasseh), and a book which warned that the only way to ensure the nation's continuing existence was unswerving faithfulness to God alone.

2 The centralization of worship, the dismantling of other orthodox Israelite shrines, the destruction of pagan shrines, and the removal of the paraphernalia of pagan religions were all actions in keeping with *Deuteronomy's* call for:

- a single shrine, Deuteronomy 12:5,11,14,18,21,26; 14:23; 16:2, etc.;
- condemnation of astral worship (17:3), Canaanite fertility cult practices and installations (16:21), and all other non-Israelite religious rites and shrines, 12:3.

3 The observance of the Passover in the Jerusalem Temple, rather than in the homes of the people, was in keeping with Deuteronomy 16:1–8. Second Kings 23:22 hints at the newness of this arrangement.

4 Second Kings 23:9 states that those priests who had been attached to outlying shrines did not go to Jerusalem; this points to a knowledge of Deuteronomy 18:6–8.

THE ORIGIN OF THE LAW BOOK

1 What was the origin of the law book, and how did it get into the Jerusalem Temple? Possibly the book was first used in the Northern Kingdom in an attempt to centralize all northern worship at a single shrine. The language of the law book is consistent with the culture and traditions of the north. One theory is that when the Northern Kingdom was destroyed by the Assyrians, priests from the north fled south bringing their oral and written traditions with them—and deposited their writings in the Jerusalem Temple.

2 If this suggestion is correct, the book must *originally* have been intended to speak to conditions in the Northern Kingdom similar to those it *eventually* spoke to during the course of Josiah's reform. Prophets had expressed sincere concern about conditions in the Northern Kingdom. They had warned about apostasy and ignorance of God's will, and stated that inhumane treatment of the poor and powerless would not go unpunished. They had warned that a multitude of shrines, feasts, and festivals would not save Israel. They had stressed the need for the people of Israel to know and do God's will. They had warned against pandering to the religious practices of foreigners.

3 Deuteronomy never attaches a name to the locality that was to serve as the central shrine. It refers to it merely as "the place where the Lord will make His name to dwell," ch. 12. One may assume that Mt. Gerizim—which is immediately south of Shechem—became that place in Israel because of its central location. John 4 states that the Samaritans of Jesus' day believed that Mt. Gerizim—not Jerusalem—was the only valid place for worship.

At the time of Josiah's reform, those who read "the book of the law" *assumed* that "the place" was Jerusalem. *If this assumption is correct, the choice of Jerusalem as the only legitimate place for worship and sacrifice in Judah was based on a guess validated by the actions of David and Hezekiah.*

4 It would have made sense to press for the centralization of worship in Israel, possibly at Shechem or on Mt. Gerizim, which in turn would have called for the destruction of all other shrines. However, the warnings of the prophets went unheeded, and the attempts by the priests to centralize Israel's worship life were ineffective.

5. During Josiah's reform measures in 621 B.C., Deuteronomy was discovered and read. Jerusalem's religious leaders now applied Deuteronomy's message to their own situation—with the result that a book that earlier spoke to a situation in the Northern Kingdom now spoke again to a similar situation in the Southern Kingdom.

6. The following Deuteronomic emphases are significant:

   a. Deuteronomy 6:4–9 insisted that the people were to worship only the Lord. Much of the book's content was designed to help the people "know" God and His will for their lives.

   b. The problems resulting from the centralization of worship at one sanctuary were anticipated. Previously, every act of killing an animal, even for food, was looked on as a religious rite. One of the requirements was that the blood let in connection with the slaughter of an animal was to be poured out on an altar as an offering to God. What was to be done if there was only one legitimate shrine in the land? Deuteronomy gives its blessing to the slaughter of animals for food in places other than the central shrine, but insists that the blood (the life principle) should be poured out on the ground, 12:15–28.

   c. Tithes and offerings were traditionally brought to the local sanctuary in the form of grains, birds, and animals. How could these things be carried or led to a central shrine? Deuteronomy says that these offerings could be sold locally, and the proceeds taken to the central shrine and used to buy substitute offerings, 14:22–29.

   d. Local *altars* served as places of refuge where those who had committed homicide could take refuge from the next-of-kin to the person killed until the nature of the killing could be established. With the closing of these local sanctuaries, *cities of refuge* were established to compensate, 19:1–13.

The Impact of Josiah's Reform

1 The reform had both short and long-term effects on the life and thought of Judah. It gave rise to an attempt to take seriously the prophetic teachings and the covenant faith. However, reform movements sanctioned by political and religious leaders and perpetuated by popular approval can have shaky foundations. Josiah's reform grew out of a political situation. It was spurred on by the nationalistic desire to be rid of foreign domination. The life-span of the *reform* was influenced by the life-span of the *political situation* that gave rise to it.

2 It is possible that Jeremiah supported the movement for a time, but then turned against it when it became a thing of external piety and self-seeking nationalism. Furthermore, the centralization of worship in Jerusalem created in people's minds a dangerous sense of well-being. They thought that their national security was guaranteed because God dwelt in their midst, Jeremiah 7:4. Even so, Jeremiah continued to hold Josiah in high esteem because of the manner in which he administered his realm, 22:15,16.

3 Deuteronomy's theology suggested that faithfulness to God would guarantee His protection and blessing, while unfaithfulness would result in hardship and misfortune. It applied this principle to all levels of society, including national well-being, stressing that disobedience would result in the loss of the land, 4:25–31; 8:19,20; 11:1–17; 28:58–68. After Josiah's reform, upheavals occurred that moved people to question the validity of that principle.

4 Although Josiah threw idolatry and false worship out of the Temple in 621 B.C., it was all back again within a short time. How do we know? The priest-become-prophet Ezekiel was taken from Jerusalem to Babylon in 597 B.C. When Ezekiel "visited" the Temple in a vision in 593 B.C., he saw within it symbols associated with the Egyptian Book of the Dead, Baal worship, and possibly the worship of heavenly bodies, Ezekiel 8.

5 Josiah's reform influenced the nature of the worship life of the postexilic community. After the return of the exiles from Babylon in 538 B.C., it was assumed without question that all worship should be centralized in Jerusalem. Because the postexilic community had no kings, the priests gained ever-increasing power and control over the people.

6 The fact that all sacrifices now had to be offered *exclusively* in the Jerusalem Temple resulted in a commercial system of animal sellers and money changers. Some suggest that, in Jesus' day, 9,000 priests and Levites served on the Temple's staff (some scholars suggest a much greater number). Furthermore, about 80 percent of people living in Jerusalem earned their living from the Temple "system"—building ventures, selling animals, changing money, providing accommodation for pilgrims, etc. Anyone who attacked Jerusalem's salvation marketing system was asking for trouble. **When Jesus eventually attacked that sin management system, it cost Him His life!**

19A In 2 Kings 22 and 23, the writer outlines the reign of King Josiah and describes his efforts to cleanse and refurbish the Jerusalem Temple. While repairs to the Temple were being carried out, a "book of the law" was found within the complex. After the book was read to the king, Josiah:

- led a covenant renewal ceremony in the vicinity of the Jerusalem Temple;

- removed from the Jerusalem Temple numerous pagan symbols and practices;

- closed all shrines in Judah—whether orthodox or pagan;

- invited all priests officiating at orthodox shrines in Judah to join the staff of the Jerusalem Temple— an invitation which apparently the priests declined to accept;

- smashed all shrines in what had been the former Northern Kingdom and killed all priests officiating at those shrines—they were not Levites!

19B Josiah ruled Judah 640–609 B.C.—but as a vassal of Assyria. When the Assyrian Empire began to crumble after the death of King Ashurbanipal in 628 B.C., Josiah sought to free his realm from Assyrian control. Some of the religious symbols Josiah had removed from the Temple were symbols of Assyrian domination over Judah. By removing and destroying them, Josiah was saying, "We will no longer submit to Assyrian control!"

After leading the covenant renewal ceremony, and dealing with religious symbols and practices in both Judah and Israel, Josiah arranged for the celebration of a Passover within Jerusalem, 2 Kings 23:21–23. The writer points out that no such Passover (with all observants gathered in *one place*) had been held since the days of the judges—possibly with Joshua 5:10–12 in mind.

19C Most likely the book found and read during the course of Josiah's Temple repair program was Deuteronomy—or a major portion of it. Deuteronomy makes frequent reference to the importance of worshiping *one God in one place*; see Unit 11.

Possibly this law book had been used in the Northern Kingdom in an attempt to centralize worship there also—perhaps on Mt. Gerizim near Shechem. However, when the destruction of Israel was imminent, the book was brought to Judah and stored in the Jerusalem Temple—where it was discovered during the time of Josiah. The book then prompted reforms in the south similar to those which had previously taken place in the north.

19D Although Josiah removed many pagan symbols from the Jerusalem Temple in 621 B.C., Ezekiel 8 suggests that some of them were returned to the Temple within a few decades. In a vision Ezekiel the priest experienced in Babylon a few years after being taken into exile there in 597 B.C., he saw in the Jerusalem Temple symbols associated with the Egyptian Book of the Dead, Baal worship, and possibly the worship of heavenly bodies.

The centralization of worship in Jerusalem had a profound effect on the life of the postexilic community. By the time of Jesus' ministry, about eighty percent of the people living in Jerusalem earned their income from activities associated with the Temple—and at least 9,000 priests served on its staff! When Jesus finally attacked those who controlled and benefited from the Temple's sin management system, He signed His death warrant, Mark 11:18.

CROSS WAYS®

2 SECTION

UNITS 11–20

From the Conquest to the Babylonian Exile

UNIT 20
Worship and War

Worship and Holy War in the Biblical Narrative

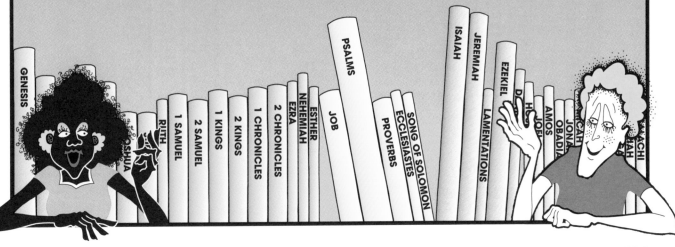

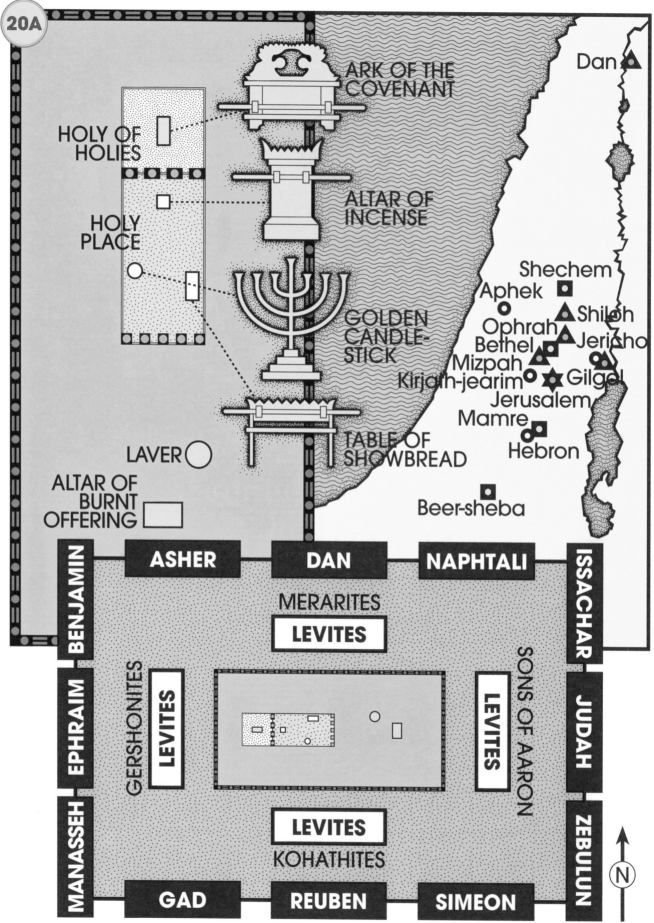

ARK OF THE COVENANT

HOLY OF HOLIES

ALTAR OF INCENSE

HOLY PLACE

GOLDEN CANDLE-STICK

LAVER

TABLE OF SHOWBREAD

ALTAR OF BURNT OFFERING

Dan

Shechem

Aphek

Ophrah   Shiloh

Bethel   Jericho

Mizpah

Kirjath-jearim   Gilgal

Jerusalem

Mamre

Hebron

Beer-sheba

BENJAMIN   ASHER   DAN   NAPHTALI   ISSACHAR

MERARITES

LEVITES

GERSHONITES   LEVITES   LEVITES   SONS OF AARON   JUDAH

EPHRAIM

MANASSEH

LEVITES

KOHATHITES

ZEBULUN

GAD   REUBEN   SIMEON

N

Patriarchal and wilderness shrines (ILLUSTRATION 20A, *top right*)

Genesis refers to the patriarchs establishing four shrines in Canaan. Usually a site was chosen, and a shrine established, after God's presence was revealed to one or more of the patriarchs there. In the illustration, *patriarchal shrines* are marked with a **square**. Shrines established *after the conquest* are marked with a **triangle**.

■ *Shechem:* Abraham's first stopping place in Canaan was Shechem. *Abraham* built an altar there to commemorate the event, Genesis 12:6,7. *Joseph's remains* were eventually brought from Egypt to Shechem for burial, Joshua 24:32. After his long years in the service of Laban, *Jacob* bought land for a campsite at Shechem and erected an altar on it, Genesis 33:18–20. The pagan images his wives brought from their homeland were ceremoniously buried there beneath an oak tree as a sign of rejection of the pagan cults associated with these images, Genesis 35:1–4.

During the time of the judges, Israel held covenant ceremonies at Shechem, Joshua 8:30–35; ch. 24. Abimelech, Gideon's son, was proclaimed king there, Judges 9:6. Rehoboam met at Shechem with representatives from the north in an effort to persuade them to accept him as their king, 1 Kings 12:1.

■ *Bethel: Abraham* established a sanctuary at Bethel, Genesis 12:8. After his vision of the stairway connecting heaven and earth, *Jacob* vowed to set up a shrine at Bethel if his venture in Haran prospered, Genesis 28:10–22. It did, and he fulfilled the vow, Genesis 35:1–9.

■ *Mamre: Abraham* stayed at Mamre and built an altar, Genesis 13:18. *Abraham, Isaac,* and *Jacob* lived there at various times. Nearby was the cave of Machpelah where the bodies of the patriarchs and their wives were buried (Abraham and Sarah, Isaac and Rebekah, Jacob and Leah; Rachel was buried in Bethlehem). Genesis 13:18, 23:19 and 35:27 identify Mamre with Hebron.

■ *Beer-sheba:* Genesis 21:33 traces the origin of the shrine at Beer-sheba to *Abraham*. God appeared to *Isaac* at Beer-sheba and repeated to him the promise previously made to Abraham, Genesis 26:23–25. God later appeared to *Jacob* in the same region, and the patriarch sacrificed there, Genesis 46:1–4.

Tabernacle (ILLUSTRATION 20A, *top left*)

The biblical materials that describe Israel's worship life during the wilderness wanderings refer to both:

- An elaborate *Tabernacle* and *ARK OF THE COVENANT* (or Presence)
- A simple *Tent of Meeting* and *Ark of the* Presence (or *Covenant*)

1 Details of the *Tabernacle*, its furnishings, and its personnel are given in Exodus 25–31 and 35–40. The central structure consisted of a rectangular wooden framework that was covered, except for its eastern entrance, with long strips of fabric joined together with hooks and eyes. Representations of cherubim were embroidered into this covering, which in turn was covered by two hard-wearing layers of skins and light leathers. It measured 45' x 15' x 15' (13.75 x 4.5 x 4.5 meters)—one cubit = 18" or 0.45 meters—and lay on an east-west axis.

2 The compartment at the *western end* was called the *HOLY OF HOLIES*; the *eastern section* was called the *HOLY PLACE*. They were separated by *four pillars and a curtain*. The opening at the eastern end was closed off with *five pillars and a curtain*. The pillars were of acacia wood covered with gold, and rested on silver bases; the entrance pillars were placed on bronze bases.

3 The *ARK OF THE COVENANT* is described as a box measuring about 4' x 2½' by 2½' (1.2 x .75 x .75 meters). It was made of acacia wood covered with gold and included rings through which carrying poles could be passed. Across its top was a solid gold slab called the *Mercy Seat*, from which God dispensed mercy to the people, Exodus 25:17–22. At each end of the Mercy Seat, and in one piece with it, stood a *cherub*. Each cherub faced the center with wings arched overhead to surround the sacred center of the Mercy Seat, Exodus 25:10–22.

Some believe that the cherubim were winged bulls similar to those used in numerous parts of Mesopotamia. Others suggest that the cherubim on the Mercy Seat were winged lions with a human head—a religious symbol used frequently in Phoenicia and Palestine. Cherubs transported a god from place to place, Psalm 18:10. In biblical usage, they were thrones for God's invisible presence. The Ark was, after all, viewed as God's throne or footstool, 1 Samuel 4:4; 2 Samuel 6:2; Psalm 99:5. Some suggest that the wings of the cherubim formed a backrest for God as He sat on His throne—which the Ark was thought to be.

4 In the Holy Place were the Altar of Incense, a golden seven-branched candlestick, and the Table of Showbread.

The Tabernacle was placed within a larger court measuring 150' x 75' (46 x 23 meters) and bordered by a system of bronze posts supporting silver rods from which hung linen drapes. In this court were the Altar for Burnt Offerings and the Laver in which the vessels used in the various rituals were washed.

5 Degrees of holiness: When the Pentateuch refers to the objects in the Tabernacle, the sequence of reference reflects the order of importance and holiness attached to each item: the Ark of the Presence in the Holy of Holies, the furniture within the Holy Place, the Tabernacle itself, the furniture in the outer court, and finally the outer enclosure. Similarly, fine gold was used at the very center of the Tabernacle, ordinary gold a little further out, then silver and bronze.

6 Cloud and fire: During the wilderness wanderings, God's presence hovered over the Tabernacle in the form of a pillar of cloud by day and a pillar of fire by night. Whenever the cloud was taken up from above the Tabernacle, the people broke camp and continued on their journey. They remained in camp while the cloud continued above the Tabernacle, Exodus 40:34–38.

7 According to Numbers 4:48, the Tabernacle was cared for by 8,580 priests and Levites.

The layout of the camp (ILLUSTRATION 20A, *lower section*)

1 *LEVITES:* The tribe of Levi, once listed among the twelve tribes, was eventually assigned a full-time priestly role, Numbers 1:47–54. The number of tribes was maintained at twelve by counting the house of Joseph as two tribes, namely *MANASSEH* and *EPHRAIM*. Moses and Aaron both belonged to the tribe of Levi.

2 Among the Levites a distinction was made between *SONS OF AARON* and *other Levites*. Aaron's descendants were to perform the chief priestly duties *in the sanctuary*. The other Levites (*MERARITES*, *GERSHONITES*, *KOHATHITES*) were to serve as priestly *assistants*. Among other things, they protected and transported the Tabernacle, Numbers 1:47–54; 2:17.

3 The Levites were positioned immediately around the outer court, Exodus 27:9–19. In this arrangement Moses, Aaron, and his sons were positioned on the eastern side. The twelve tribes were to camp further out, three on each side, in a rectangular layout. *JUDAH* occupied the center of the *east side*, *EPHRAIM* the center of the *west side*, *REUBEN* the center of the *south side*, and *DAN* the center of the *north side*. Each gave its name to the side of the camp in which it was located.

The Tent of Meeting (not depicted in ILLUSTRATION 20A)

Exodus 39:32–40:38 weaves together Tent of Meeting and Tabernacle traditions without explanatory comment.

1 The *Tent of Meeting* is mentioned in relation to events in the vicinity of Mt. Sinai (Exodus 33:7–11) and Kadesh-barnea, Numbers 11:16–17, 24–26; 12:4. According to these passages, the Tent of Meeting was a simple structure which Moses pitched from time to time outside the camp. God met with Moses there (hence, Tent of *Meeting*). During Moses' absence, Joshua cared for it.

2 In Deuteronomy 10:1–5, God commands Moses to meet Him on Mt. Sinai, and make two preparations. *First*, Moses is to make two tablets of stone similar to those he broke after Israel's worship of the golden calf. *Second*, he is to make an Ark of acacia wood into which he is to place the tablets of stone after descending from the mountain top. Moses attends to all these details. This passage suggests that the *Ark of the Presence/Covenant* was a simple object and contained only the law tablets, see also 1 Kings 8:9. However, Numbers 17:10 says Aaron's rod was kept near or in it; Exodus 16:33 says a container of manna was placed within it.

3 There is debate as to what the tent used during the wilderness period looked like. Some believe that the Pentateuch's description of the Tabernacle and the Ark of the Presence is idealized.

An interesting insight emerges when one notes what some Jewish teachers taught about the origin of the *Pentateuch*, Genesis–Deuteronomy. They taught that the first thing God created was the Pentateuch—which He did hundreds and even thousand of years before He created the universe. The Pentateuch remained in God's mind until He eventually dictated it, word by word, to Moses at Sinai. However, if it existed long before creation (and served as the blueprint on which creation was based), then God planned the Tabernacle long before He created the universe.

If the Tabernacle's measurements were approximately half those of Solomon's Temple, then the Tabernacle might be understood as a *proposed preliminary model* for Solomon's Temple. The implication then is that the Jerusalem Temple was a very holy structure—*God designed it long before He created the universe.*

Beyond the wilderness wanderings (ILLUSTRATION 20A, *top right*)

The last *clear* mention of the *Tent of Meeting* occurs in Numbers 25:6, which states that it was set up in the plains of Moab—the last stopping place east of the Jordan prior to the conquest.

No *clear* reference is made to the **Tabernacle** after Israel enters Canaan. One wonders why. After all, scholars who have analyzed the biblical text very carefully suggest that the Tabernacle structure contained 1¼ tons of gold, 4 tons of silver, 3 tons of bronze, precious stones, and hundreds of feet of curtain. It is hard to believe that Israel would have left it in the wilderness.

1 After the entry into the Promised Land, the **Ark of the Covenant** was kept at **Gilgal** ⬢ (Joshua 4:15–19; 7:6), then **Bethel** ◻ (Judges 20:18), **Shiloh** ⬢ (1 Samuel 3:3), and apparently *Nob*, 1 Samuel 21:1–6.

2 The sanctuary at **Shiloh** ◻ seems to have been a substantial building. It is called *the temple of the Lord* (1 Samuel 1:9), *the house of the Lord* (1 Samuel 1:24), and *the tent of meeting* (1 Samuel 2:22), and has doors, 1 Samuel 3:15. 1 Samuel 14:18 says Saul used to take the Ark of the Covenant with him into battle.

3 According to 1 Samuel 4:1–7:2, after the Philistines captured the Ark in a battle at **Aphek**, they eventually sent it back to Israel. It was kept at **Kiriath-jearim** until David brought it from there to **Jerusalem** and placed it into a tent which he built for it, 2 Samuel 6. Eventually Solomon placed it into the Holy of Holies of his Temple, 1 Kings 6:19, 8:1–9.

4 The **Ark of the Covenant** then served as the central focus of Israelite worship until the Babylonians destroyed Jerusalem and plundered the Temple in 587 B.C. The Ark then disappeared from history.

5 The **Holy of Holies** in the Temple, built by those who returned from exile, was empty except for a low square stone in the center of the floor—a stone which the rabbis equated with the one Jacob used as a pillow at Bethel, Genesis 28. This *foundation stone* (as it was called) served as the link between heaven and earth, and between God and humanity. Jesus eventually made the radical claim that He replaced that stone and its function, John 1:51.

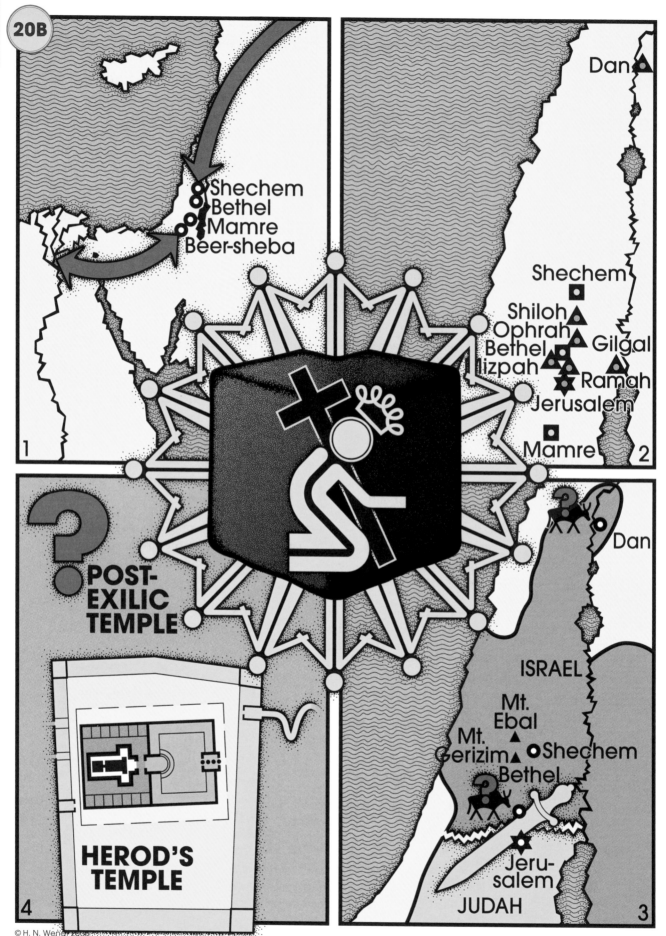

20B

1

Shechem
Bethel
Mamre
Beer-sheba

2

Dan

Shechem

Shiloh
Ophrah
Bethel
Mizpah
Gilgal
Ramah

Jerusalem

Mamre

4

POST-EXILIC TEMPLE

HEROD'S TEMPLE

3

Dan

ISRAEL

Mt. Ebal
Mt. Gerizim
Shechem
Bethel

Jeru-salem

JUDAH

The numbers below correspond to those in **ILLUSTRATION 20B**.

OLD TESTAMENT

1 The patriarchs established worship sites at **Shechem**, **Bethel**, **Mamre**, and **Beer-sheba**.

2 ▪ Three worship sites originally established by the patriarchs, and reestablished after the conquest.

▲ Worship sites established after the conquest.

Although Deuteronomy insisted that the people should worship *one God in one place* (see Units 11 and 19), Exodus 20:24 permitted the Israelites to build numerous shrines in the Promised Land after the conquest.

▲ **Dan:** The origin of the sanctuary at Dan is described in Judges 17,18; see Unit 13.

▲ **Gilgal:** Gilgal was the Israelites' first stopping place after they crossed the Jordan River. See Joshua 4:15–19.

▲ **Shiloh:** Eventually Shiloh replaced Gilgal as the focal point of worship in Israel. It was used as a meeting place for all the tribes, Joshua 18:1; 21:2; 22:9,12. The Ark was kept there (1 Samuel 3), but eventually made its way to Kiriath-jearim, 1 Samuel 4:1–7:2; see Unit 14.

▲ **Mizpah:** A center of worship during the time of the judges (Judges 20:1,3; 21:1,5,8) and during the time of Samuel, 1 Samuel 7:5–12, 10:17–24.

▲ **Ophrah:** Referred to as a shrine in Judges 6:11–32.

✡ **Jerusalem:** Plays a central role throughout the biblical narrative; 2 Samuel 5:6–10, ch. 6; 2 Samuel 24:18–20; 2 Chronicles 3:1; 1 Kings 8. The first Temple is built in Jerusalem by Solomon soon after he came to power in 960 B.C.

3 After Solomon's death and the division of the realm, Jeroboam set up shrines at **Dan** and **Bethel** as rivals to the Jerusalem Temple, 1 Kings 12:29; see Unit 1. Although 1 and 2 Kings attack these shrines as idolatrous (**calves**), it is possible they were not (**question marks**) and that the issue had to do with *geographical validity* rather than *theological orthodoxy*.

There is reason to believe that prior to the destruction of the Northern Kingdom by the Assyrians in 721 B.C., an attempt was made to centralize worship in the Northern Kingdom, possibly on **Mt. Gerizim** near **Shechem**. The book of Deuteronomy may have originated at this time and in this place.

As a result of Josiah's reform in 621 B.C., **Jerusalem** became the only place where people might offer sacrifice, with the result that its Temple eventually gained prestige, power, and influence.

4 Nothing is known about the **POSTEXILIC TEMPLE** dedicated in 515 B.C. Herod the Great demolished it in 19 B.C., and then began work on a much more elaborate structure. **HEROD'S TEMPLE** was completed in A.D. 63, but destroyed by the Romans in A.D. 70.

NEW TESTAMENT

Center section

Jesus did not attack the Temple itself. He attacked the abuses taking place within it (Mark 11:15–17), and said that He is to be seen as a replacement of the structure and its system, John 1:51, 2:13–22. **Jesus' Temple is a community of people among whom He dwells.** He, the **Servant-King** of that community, is the **cornerstone** of the new spiritual Temple structure, the new Temple **community**. Jesus' desire is to give *servant shape* to the lives of those "living stones" joined *to Him* in saving faith and *to each other* in servant fellowship, Ephesians 2:19–22.

Holy War

OVERVIEW

ILLUSTRATION 20C traces stages in the understanding of Holy War through the sweep of the biblical narrative. The numbers below correspond to those in the illustration.

1 **Exodus, Conquest, Judges** (**ILLUSTRATION 12A** in miniature)

Holy War played its most significant role during the Exodus and wilderness wanderings (Units 7 and 10), the conquest (Unit 12), and the time of the judges (Unit 13). In the biblical materials that deal with these periods, God is often pictured as a Warrior God who leads the Israelites in a Holy War against their enemies. The Exodus from Egypt was understood as God's defeat of the pharaoh and his forces in order to lead Israel to freedom. God fought for Israel because God loved and cared for Israel. Although Joshua and the various judges led the people into battle, they were merely the visible agents of Israel's invisible God.

2 **The Period of the Monarchy** (*crowns*, *fortress*, *David's campaigns*; see **ILLUSTRATION 15A**)

Although the traditional understanding of Holy War persisted during the time of Saul, when David came to the throne, the tribal organization in Israel diminished in significance. Under Solomon, it vanished. Now victory depended not on the presence, direction, and power of God, but on military might, fortresses, and human strategies. Kings waged wars to serve the interests of national policies. Only lip service was paid to the older traditions. Although the king sought God's counsel before going into battle, the prophets he consulted were often creatures of the court who pandered to the king's whim; see 1 Kings 22, and note vv. 5,6. Rare and courageous was the person who dared stand up against the king, 1 Kings 22:13–23. To guarantee national security, rulers looked to international treaties rather than to God's power, 1 Kings 15:18,19; 16:31; 2 Kings 15:19; 16: 5–9; 17:4.

3 **Holy War and the Prophets** (*roaring lion*, Hosea 13:7,8; *Assyria*, Isaiah 10:5; *Babylon*, Jeremiah 27:6; *Egypt*, Micah 1:10–16)

Prophets such as Elijah and Elisha did not oppose war. On the contrary, they and other earlier prophets engaged in stirring up internal unrest, or in encouraging the king in his military undertakings, 1 Kings 1:11–14; 11:29–39; 16:1–4; 18:17; 2 Kings 9; 1 Kings 20:22–25, 26–28; 2 Kings 3:13–20; 6:11,12. King Joash referred to Elisha as "the chariots of Israel and its horsemen," 2 Kings 13:14. Elisha died condemning the king for not wishing to strike down the Syrians more than three times, 2 Kings 13:14–19.

The literary prophets sometimes backed the king in his plans for war, but more often they opposed war. They did this not because they thought Holy War to be a thing of the past (indeed, they insisted it was the only valid kind of war), but because *grounds for such a war were entirely lacking in Israel.* The people could engage in Holy War only if they demonstrated an unshakable trust in the Lord. But they did not. They trusted in wealth, military might, alliances with foreign powers, and in political scheming and compromise, Isaiah 30:1–5; 31:1; Jeremiah 9:23; 17:5; Amos 2:13–16; Hosea 7:11.

Israel had abandoned or corrupted the worship of God and embraced the gods of neighboring nations. Therefore, the idea that God was still with Israel was unthinkable. Israel was no longer God's special covenant people separated from other nations of the earth. The people had entangled themselves with those other nations (Hosea 7:8), and therefore stood under judgment. Accordingly, Israel would be caught up in the military campaigns of neighboring nations that aspired for political grandeur and would become a spoil of war. God would even use other nations to fight against His own people, and bring divine judgment on them, Isaiah 5:26–30; 10:5–11; Jeremiah 5:29–6:5; Hosea 10:7–10; Amos 3:12; Micah 1:10–16; Habakkuk 1:15–17. To resist the advancing armies of Assyria and Babylon was to resist God!

4 **Postexilic Period**

After the return from Babylon in 538 B.C., Holy War was viewed as the instrument God would use to bring down retribution on the nations that made life difficult for His people. Hints of this occur already before the deportations of the people of Judah to exile in Babylon in 597 and 587 B.C. God was sovereign over all nations and all history! God was the One who punished evil wherever it appeared, Amos 1:1–2:3. After the exile, God would punish in particular those nations that had oppressed His people, Jeremiah 46:10; Obadiah 14; Nahum 1:2,3. God could even make use of foreign powers to make it possible for His people to return from exile, Isaiah 45:1.

Old Testament writings contain a number of lists of (often, *seven*) nations that the Israelites despised. Seven such nations are referred to in Genesis 12–50, Deuteronomy 7:1, Joshua 3:10, Ezekiel 25–32. According to Mark, when Jesus fed the 4,000 in the Decapolis (non-Jewish, *Gentile* territory), there were *seven* baskets of left-overs! Jesus had compassion for the Gentiles!

5. Jesus the Messiah

In the New Testament, Holy War is viewed differently. God's people do not struggle against national, political foes; they struggle against the realm of the demonic (**satanic face inside symbol for sin**). Their weapons are spiritual, to be used against the powers of evil. The Gospel according to St. Mark presents Jesus' ministry as a battle against the demonic, 1:12,13; 3:22–27; 4:35–5:20. The Christian is to see life as a lifelong battle against the powers of Satan, a seductive world order, and the sinful human spirit, 1 Corinthians 14:8; 2 Corinthians 10:3; Ephesians 6:10–18; 1 Timothy 1:18,19.

PREPARATIONS FOR HOLY WAR

1. When Israel was contemplating a war, it was essential that God should approve of, and participate in, what was planned, Deuteronomy 20. Rituals were practiced prior to any battle to ensure God's help. These rituals consisted of interpreting dreams, making use of Urim and Thummim (objects used by priests for divination), or seeking the word of a prophet, Judges 7:9–14; 1 Samuel 28:6, 30:7; 2 Samuel 5:19,23; 1 Kings 22:5,7,8. Even while the battle was being waged, God's advice was sought concerning the strategy to be employed, 2 Samuel 5:19–25. Those who sought this advice from God brought with them sacrifices and offerings, 1 Samuel 7:9.

2. On occasion, leaders summoned Israel's fighting men together for battle by means of a rite in which an ox was cut into pieces. The pieces were sent far and wide to the various tribal groups, 1 Samuel 11:7. Judges 19:29 states that after the Benjaminites ravished a Levite's concubine, portions of the woman's body were used instead of portions of an animal.

3. The Holy War could be either *offensive* or *defensive*. The battles Israel fought under the leadership of Joshua were *offensive*. Those they fought to repel any foreign power that dared invade their territory were *defensive*.

PARTICIPANTS IN THE HOLY WAR

1. The real leader in the wars Israel waged was God. Those who led Israel into battle were placed into their position by a special outpouring of the spirit of God. Their authority depended on this circumstance and not on their own ability, Judges 6:34, 11:29. If for some reason the spirit of God was withdrawn from them, they lost their authority to lead, Judges 16:20; 1 Samuel 16:14.

2. Soldiers who took part in a Holy War were required to dedicate themselves completely to the task of fighting for God and Israel. *They were serving God in what they were doing.* Those who were not in a position to apply themselves wholeheartedly to fighting were invited to withdraw from the campaign and return to their homes. Among these were the timid, the newly wed, and those distracted by family and financial worries, Deuteronomy 20:5–9. Their continuing presence would have diminished the effectiveness of the larger group, Judges 5:2.

3 The blessing of the religious leaders and priests was sought for any Holy War undertaken, Deuteronomy 20:2; 1 Samuel 10:1. Soldiers who took part in a campaign were seen as "holy persons" throughout the time of the campaign, 1 Samuel 21:4; Isaiah 13:3. The military camps had to be kept ritually clean; they were places in which God "walked," Deuteronomy 23:14. Human wastes had to be buried outside the boundaries of the camp, Deuteronomy 23:12,13. Any soldier who experienced a bodily discharge had to undergo a period of purification outside the camp limits, Deuteronomy 23:10,11. Sexual intercourse was forbidden during a Holy War. Soldiers who failed to observe this requirement disqualified themselves from entry into the camp, 1 Samuel 21:4; 2 Samuel 11:11.

THE CONDUCT OF THE HOLY WAR

1 God led the people into battle, fought for them, and gave them the victory, Exodus 14:14; Deuteronomy 20:4; Judges 4:14. Various battle cries expressed this: "The Lord has delivered them into our hand," Judges 3:28; 7:15; 1 Samuel 7:8; Joshua 2:14. In the final analysis, the Holy War was the Lord's war, 1 Samuel 18:17; 25:28. It therefore did not matter how many soldiers were in the army fighting a Holy War, Judges 7; 1 Samuel 14:6. The final outcome of any campaign did not depend on the number of Israelite soldiers. It depended on God.

2 The call to assemble and attack was given by means of a blast on a *shofar*, or ram's horn, Numbers 10:9; 31:6; Judges 3:27; 1 Samuel 13:3. At the crucial moment in a battle, the terror of the Lord would fall on the enemy and throw them into confusion. All that Israel's armies had to do was mop up after God had won the battle for them, Joshua 10:10; Judges 4:15; 1 Samuel 7:10; 2 Samuel 5:24.

3 Holy War thinking was not confined to Israel. It found a place in all nations in the Ancient Near East. Wars were thought of as struggles between the national gods of the respective nations, 1 Samuel 4:7; 1 Kings 20:28; 2 Kings 18:28–35. On the occasion when the Philistines defeated Israel at the battle of Aphek, they captured the Ark of the Covenant and placed it before a statue of their god Dagon in one of their temples. However, the reader is given the subtle hint that the Philistine victory was not really proof of any superior power on the part of Dagon, for Dagon fell on his face before the Ark and broke into pieces, 1 Samuel 5:1–5. On occasion, when things were not going well, human sacrifice could be employed to stir up the national deity to greater heights of achievement. According to 2 Kings 3:21–27, the king of Moab offered up his son as a burnt offering during the course of a battle with the armies of Israel, Judah, and Edom.

THE OUTCOME OF A HOLY WAR (Deuteronomy 20:10–20)

When a city *outside Israel's borders* was being attacked it was offered terms of peace. If the city accepted these terms, its citizens were enslaved but not put to death. If the city rejected the terms of peace, its *men* were put to death, but its *women and children* were spared. The city's contents were considered legitimate spoil for the attackers.

If the city being attacked was *within Israel's borders*, it was to be placed under the ban and completely destroyed. It was set on fire and offered up in flames as an offering to the Lord.

AFTER THE BATTLE

The Holy War was never fought for its own sake. Those who fought it looked beyond the day of battle to the peace which would come when the fighting came to an end. The war was necessary only to make it possible for God's people to attain those conditions of tranquility and prosperity that were thought to be part of the all-embracing dream of eventual peace. When the fighting was over, and all proper procedures and rituals attended to, the cry went up, "To the tents, O Israel," Joshua 22:4,8; Judges 20:8.

20A ● Throughout their history, the Israelites showed much interest in where and how to worship. At stake were the presence of God in their midst and the perpetuation of life in the Promised Land. The Genesis narrative speaks of the patriarchs establishing, and worshiping at, shrines in:

Shechem (Abraham and Jacob)
Bethel (Abraham and Jacob)
Mamre (Abraham, Isaac, and Jacob)
Beer-sheba (Abraham, Isaac, and Jacob)

● Although the narratives describing the wilderness wanderings devote much attention to descriptions of worship structures and the sacred objects used within them, it is difficult to harmonize some of the details. For example, although the biblical text describes a *simple* Tent of Meeting and Ark of the Presence, it also describes an *elaborate* Tabernacle and Ark of the Covenant.

● During their stay at Mt. Sinai, the people constructed a portable shrine which was located at the center of the community whenever the Israelites set up camp. A variety of sacred objects was housed within it. The Levites were allocated places close to it, and the twelve tribes were to set up camp around it—three tribes per side. The Levites carried the shrine and its contents during the period of the wilderness wanderings.

20B ● The locations of the shrines established by the patriarchs (Shechem, Bethel, Mamre, and Beer-sheba) continued to play an important role throughout the Old Testament narrative.

● There is no clear reference to the Tabernacle being erected in the Promised Land after the people crossed the Jordan. However, reference is made to the Ark's presence in a number of locations, e.g. Shiloh, 1 Samuel 3. David eventually transferred the Ark from Kiriath-jearim to Jerusalem and placed it into a tent; Solomon placed it in the Temple he built to house it.

● When, after Solomon's death, the United Kingdom split, Jeroboam I established shrines in the Northern Kingdom at Bethel and Dan—which angered those who lived in Judah and Jerusalem.

● The Babylonians destroyed the Jerusalem Temple and the Ark of the Covenant in 587 B.C. Little is known about the postexilic Temple. In 19 B.C., Herod began building a magnificent Temple that was completed in A.D. 63, but destroyed by the Romans in A.D. 70.

● Although Jesus did not attack the Temple itself during His ministry, He attacked the abuses that were taking place within it. Jesus declared that the building *in Jerusalem* made of stones would be replaced by a *world-wide* spiritual structure of *living stones joined to Him (the Cornerstone of God's new spiritual Temple-community) in faith and servanthood.*

20C At no stage in their history could the Israelites boast, "This is what *we* have accomplished!" On the contrary, they could only confess, "This is what *the Lord* has done for us." The Lord Himself engaged in the Israelites' battles and achieved victory for them. Five stages emerge in the history of Holy War within the life of Israel.

● *During the Exodus and conquest:* The Lord fought for the Israelites.

● *During the period of the monarchy:* Waging war was undertaken to expand the nation's borders.

● *In the oracles of the pre-exilic prophets:* God declared war on His own people because they had forgotten His covenant relationship with them. God led foreign armies against Israel because, although the people did not take the covenant seriously, He did!

● *The postexilic period:* The belief was that God would pour out His wrath on those nations that had harassed and destroyed Israel and Judah.

● *Jesus the Messiah:* Holy War was—and continues to be—the battle between the Kingdom of God and the Kingdom of Satan.

A Question of Sources

The *Crossways* materials are designed to help people understand and interpret the *biblical* materials, and to provide a tool to enable teachers and students to work together to unravel and interpret the Bible's complex narrative. Those who undertake theological studies in many seminaries today know that one of the first things they are exposed to in biblical studies is the "historical-critical method" and the question of sources in the Pentateuchal materials. Some comments are in order.

First, it might be argued that the term historical-critical is an unfortunate one, for it gives the impression that the goal of scholars is to criticize the text. Perhaps it would be better to speak of the historical-*analytical* method.

Second, one of the unfortunate things that happens in some seminaries is that students spend a lot of time taking the biblical text apart, but not much time putting it together. The goal of the *Crossways* materials is to help people put the biblical text together—to gain an oversight of the biblical narrative as a whole. Unless students do that, they run the risk of dehistoricizing Jesus and lifting Him out of the context of Judaism.

What follows is designed to help those who may never darken the door of a seminary understand what biblical scholars have in mind when they refer to *sources* in the Pentateuch. It makes sense to deal with the matter at this point in the materials—after students have had a chance to think through the biblical narrative from creation to the Babylonian exile.

Scholars refer to four major sources in Genesis through Deuteronomy, and define their origins as follows:

 ### The Jahwist (J)

This source was written in Judah, probably Jerusalem, possibly during the reign of Solomon or one of his immediate successors. That means it was written in the late tenth or early ninth century B.C. Its goal was to show that the promises made to Abraham were fulfilled in David's kingdom. It uses the name *Jahweh* when referring to God. It looks with favor on strong leaders like David, and on Jerusalem and its Temple.

 ### The Elohist (E)

After Solomon's death and the division of the realm, the Northern Kingdom needed its own version of history—a version that reflected an anti-Jerusalem bias. The suggestion is that this version was written after 900 B.C. It prefers the name *Elohim* for God, places much emphasis on the importance of northern locations such as Bethel and Shechem, and gives prominence to the tribe and territory of Ephraim. Both Joshua and Jeroboam I were from Ephraim.

The Deuteronomist (D)

The theory is that the Deuteronomic materials were produced in the eighth and seventh centuries B.C. They assess the Jahwist and Elohist histories in relation to pagan influences on the faith life of the people and the religious track-records of the northern and southern kings. The Deuteronomist agrees that the Sinai covenant was more important than kingship, and stresses the importance of total loyalty to the God of the patriarchs. Although Deuteronomy might have been used originally to encourage the centralization of worship in Israel at Shechem or Gerizim, the Deuteronomist who produced 1 and 2 Kings agrees with the Jahwist that Jerusalem was to be the only center for worship after the destruction of the Northern Kingdom in 721 B.C.

 ### The Priestly source (P)

It is thought that the Priestly materials were produced some time after those of the Deuteronomist. They were put together in a way that showed a concern for the needs of the community in exile in

Babylon. They place great emphasis on obedience to the law, stress the importance of personal commitment to God, and assure the people that God will continue to bless them no matter how desperate their situation. Most likely, they played an important role in defining worship life and ritual purity in the postexilic period—a period when the daily life of God's people was determined and guided by the religious leaders serving at the Jerusalem Temple.

The J and E versions of history existed side by side until the destruction of the Northern Kingdom in 721 B.C. Some northern priests then fled south to Judah and took their sacred writings with them. Some time later, the J and E versions were woven together to form a single account. After Judah went into exile in 587 B.C., the D and P materials were combined with the JE document to form JEDP, today's Pentateuch. Possibly it was this final work that Ezra shared with the people some time after they returned from exile, Nehemiah 8,9.

Those who wish to know more about this issue of sources are referred to Richard Elliott Friedman's insightful work, *Who Wrote the Bible* (New York, N.Y., Harper and Row, 1989). However, in the final analysis, all students of the Bible, whether clergy or layperson, must strive to saturate themselves in the biblical text that the Holy Spirit has seen fit to give us, and ask constantly, "What in heaven's name is going on here, what on earth does it mean, and what does it say to God's people today?"